Little Known

HEALTH
REMEDIES

Based on the latest
medical and scientific discoveries
for the treatment and prevention of disease
and everyday ailments

By
Bill Habets

First published in Great Britain in 1994
by Carnell Limited
37 Salisbury House, London Wall, London EC2M 5PJ

Copyright © 1994 by Carnell Limited

Typeset by Bob Loats Design
8 Frenchgate Road, Eastbourne, East Sussex

Printed in England by Clays Ltd, St Ives plc

ISBN 1 85779 273 4

Important Note

This book contains information based on the latest scientific discoveries in medicine and allied fields. It also incorporates specific suggestions and advice on how to both treat and prevent many diseases and common everyday ailments.

It must, however, be pointed out that although this information is based on the views of doctors, specialists and other health professionals, individuals vary, and therefore cannot be properly advised other than by personal examination. It is therefore essential that you always get specific advice from your own doctor or qualified medical practitioner before starting any course of treatment, trying a new diet, engaging in any kind of exercise programme, or if symptoms of illness manifest themselves.

A book like this one cannot be – nor is it intended to be – in any way a substitute for professional medical opinion. Only your own doctor or qualified medical practitioner can help you decide what may or may not be indicated, appropriate or helpful in the specific circumstances of your own individual case. Nevertheless, being aware of other possible treatments or approaches can be extremely useful to you as this will allow you to understand your own condition more fully and so perhaps deal with it better.

Introduction

This book contains vital health information provided by the top experts in their respective fields, doctors, specialists, surgeons and consultants. Within these pages you will find full details of the newest approaches to both treating and preventing a wide variety of ailments, based upon the latest research and findings emanating from medical schools, universities, learned bodies and research institutes, both in this country and abroad.

Medical knowledge is nowadays increasing at an enormous rate. While this tremendous advance in scientific understanding is good news for patients, it also means that the amount of new information becoming available every year is so vast that it can be extremely difficult to keep up to date. In fact, the most dedicated of doctors and general practitioners will often candidly admit that there just aren't enough hours in the day to allow them to absorb all the recent research they ideally should. Naturally enough, to keep abreast of the latest developments is yet more difficult for patients, especially as many of the researchers' findings are only published in comparatively obscure specialist journals.

This book's purpose is to help fill that information gap by presenting the most relevant of recent medical findings. In particular, it concentrates on those subjects where current research has shown a new way of treating or preventing specific ailments as this is the information that is most likely to be directly helpful to any reader interested in preserving their health or ensuring that they are getting the best possible treatment.

Finally, it needs to be stressed that while the views and opinions of the top international experts quoted in this book are extremely important, these pronouncements are, of course, no substitute for getting advice from your own doctor or qualified medical practitioner as they are the only ones who can determine exactly what is best for you in the specific circumstances of your own case.

Bill Habets

AIR TRAVEL

• How to beat AIRPLANE EAR

The changes in air pressure that take place even when flying in pressurised aircraft can create extremely uncomfortable symptoms for many passengers. An expert on the subject is Dr James Donaldson, professor emeritus of otolaryngology at the University of Washington School of Medicine, who offers these tips to help you avoid any problems when flying:

• If at all possible, try not to fly when you have a cold or the flu because upper respiratory infections affect your eustachian tubes and these may be unable to cope with the vacuum created by the aircraft's descent and allow germs to be sucked into your middle ear.

• Repeated swallowing and yawning are very effective at equalising pressure. But, if you're starting to feel really uncomfortable, supplement these by taking a deep breath, holding your nose, shutting your mouth tightly, puffing out your cheeks and blowing firmly.

• This is a technique often used by aircrew and known as the 'pilot's ear pop': Once again pinch your nostrils shut with one hand, take in some air, and puff out both cheeks. Then use the fingers of your free hand to push in your cheeks thereby forcing the air to the back of your nose while swallowing. If you've done this correctly, your success should be marked by a loud pop in the ears . . .

as well as substantial relief.

• Although not quite as effective as any of the above, chewing a stick of gum can also help open your eustachian tubes.

ALCOHOL

• Make mine a treble!

The fact that alcohol can help reduce the chances of a heart attack has been known and accepted by the medical profession for some time now, but it has always been assumed that the drink should be taken 'in moderation', this last phrase indicating no more than the equivalent of two glasses of wine a day.

Researchers at Harvard Medical School have now found that the 'moderate' limit is more like THREE glasses of wine and that people who drank up to that amount had higher levels of HDL, the type of cholesterol that protects against heart problems, and were 45 per cent less likely to have a cardiac attack than teetotallers.

Three glasses of wine is approximately equal in alcohol content to a triple whisky or one and a half pints of beer.

• Don't drink to forget – it won't work

There's no point in drinking to forget your troubles – in fact, alcohol can even strengthen painful memories.

Alcohol actually helps you

remember more clearly events that occurred just before you started drinking, say researchers at the University of North Dakota, who found that people who drank just after hearing a story were able to recall more of its details with greater clarity the following day than others who hadn't drank any alcohol.

• Here's why beer can give you a big belly

A beer belly is your body's way of telling you that you're drinking too much and this stops it from burning the fat away quickly enough.

Swiss researchers have found that when people drink alcohol their bodies are less efficient than usual at burning up fat. And, fat that isn't burned off, ends up being stored in the midriff, thighs or other places where people tend to put on weight. So it isn't just the calories in alcoholic drinks that make them fattening, but also the way that alcohol interferes with the body's normal disposal of fat.

• Face-cream substance may repair alcohol damage

A simple substance found in many face-creams may prevent – and even reverse – brain damage resulting from drinking too much alcohol.

Gamma-linolenic acid (GLA), which is found in the oil of the evening primrose plant, has prevented damage to the brain cell membranes of 'alcoholic' rats in experiments at University College Hospital in Galway, Eire. Explained Dr Brian Leonard: "In several years of tests, we have established that a dose of GLA taken either before or after drinking has stopped the breakdown of cell membranes in rats and even repair some of the damage already done. We believe that the GLA produces unsaturated fats, which are important to maintaining the structure of the membranes, and enables these fats to adhere to the membranes and protect them."

However, don't rush off to buy evening primrose oil – which is used in many face-creams to banish blemishes and is also used in health foods as a supplement – because its brain-protecting effects haven't yet been tested on humans.

ALLERGIES

• What comes first? Shyness or allergies?

A study of 375 students from universities across America has shown that the more shy a person is the greater are the chances that he or she is also suffering from allergies, particularly hay fever.

The students surveyed were divided in four groups – from the extremely shy to the extremely outgoing – and the allergy rate was found to increase exactly to match the shyness factor. One point, however, remains unanswered: are shy people more likely to develop allergies – or are allergy sufferers more likely to be shy?

• Is your carpet making you ill?

If you've had new carpeting installed recently it's possible that it may be adversely affecting your health, say researchers in the United States.

Health problems – which may manifest themselves as rashes, nosebleeds, or flu-like symptoms – are more likely to happen if the adhesive which was used to apply the latex backing on the carpet contains a chemical called 4-PC, claim the researchers. This chemical can liberate gas fumes which are completely harmless to most people, but which can affect some who are susceptible to them. "Their bodies can't handle the gas," explains Dr Bill Hirzy, a top scientist at the Environmental Protection Agency (EPA) in the United States which is investigating whether 4-PC is indeed responsible for the varied illnesses that many thousands of people have reported after installing new carpets.

Somewhat ironically, the potential dangers of new carpeting first became known when dozens of workers at EPA headquarters became ill after new carpeting was laid down. Since then thousands of others have said that they became sick after getting new carpets.

There are several ways in which you can protect yourself from any possible dangers and Dr Hirzy recommends the following:
• Before you commit yourself to buying a latex-backed carpet, get a sample of it and keep this near you for a couple of days or so. If this makes you feel at all sick, choose another type of floor covering instead.
• Insist that the carpet layer unrolls the new carpeting fully and allows it to air for one to three days before it comes into your home, thereby allowing most of the potential fumes to evaporate first.

ANGER

• Beware of the wife who bottles up her anger

Women who suppress their anger instead of giving vent to it can seriously damage not only their own health, but that of their husbands' as well.

According to a recent US study of 192 couples, nine out of twelve men who died from cancer had been married to women who 'bottled up their anger and suppressed their emotions'. The effect of men who suppressed anger upon their wives' cancer toll was similar, but to a much lesser degree.

Explained Dr Mara Julius, of the University of Michigan: "Suppressed emotions can cause changes in the balance of our daily routines and these disrupted patterns may also influence the immune system in its vigilance against cancer." As to why men were more affected, the researchers said that this was probably because generally a husband depends more on his wife for support – and that this may have been frequently withheld if she was bottling up anger or resentment.

ANOREXIA

• The aspirin cure for ANOREXIA NERVOSA?

A special kind of treatment that affects hormone levels can cure anorexia nervosa, the eating and slimming disorder that makes people starve themselves, say researchers.

It has been found that anorexia is often accompanied by excess levels in the brain of the hormone cortisol, according to psychiatrist James Parsons, of the Alpha Medical Clinic, in Melbourne, Florida, USA. "By using drugs that lowered the level of cortisol we managed to completely reverse the self starvation habits of 60 anorexics," he said. The drugs used were several-times-a-day low doses of intravenously administered vitamin C; dilantin, an anti-convulsant; cimetidine, which is used to treat ulcers; tryptophan, an essential amino acid; and even plain aspirin, all of which were found to lower cortisol levels.

"This treatment is going to revolutionise the treatment of anorexia nervosa," claimed Dr Parsons. "Most of our patients were eating normally again within a week. More importantly, we have shown that anorexia has a biological basis – and that proper medication will correct it."

Cortisol – which is also called 'hydrocortisone' – is the major glucocorticoid synthetised and released by the human adrena cortex and is known to play a vital role in carbohydrate metabolism and for the normal response to any stress.

APHRODISIACS

• Tree bark love potion really works

Science may have finally discovered a love potion that really works, according to researchers who are about to start testing on humans a natural aphrodisiac that drove rats into a frenzy during laboratory experiments.

The amazing drug is yohimbine, a substance derived from the bark of a tropical tree, which has long been known as a folk remedy for sexual tiredness, but whose efficacy had hitherto been dismissed by doctors as a quack potion.

However, recent studies have shown that yohimbine injected into male rats did drastically increase their sex drive within 20 minutes of receiving the drug.

"This is the most powerful drug yet tested for stimulating sexual behaviour in rats," commented Dr

Erla Smith, one of the team of scientists at Stanford Medical School in Palo Alto, California, that spent four years researching yohimbine's effects. "We still don't exactly know how the drug works but we believe it boosts the effects of a chemical in the body called norepinephrine that helps the brain cells send messages to each other and also controls the sex urge." Another member of the team, Dr Julian Davidson, added that rats provided an excellent model for certain biological aspects of human sexual behaviour, including libido, but cautioned that it was too soon to say whether the love drug will work as well on humans as it has on rats. "We'll know a lot more when we've tried it on humans as we're about to do soon with an initial study involving 40 men with sexual problems."

APPENDIX

• Hang on to your appendix!

It used to be that doctors might remove a healthy appendix while performing other surgery on the assumption that this would automatically prevent it from causing trouble later.

But there is now a good reason to keep your appendix if possible, according to the British Journal of Medicine, because the otherwise useless organ provides a handy supply of tissue should reconstructive surgery ever be needed. Because of its shape, the appendix is particularly suited for rebuilding the Fallopian tubes or the biliary tract, but it can also be used in many other procedures.

ARTHRITIS

• How to beat arthritis pain while working in the garden

You can overcome pain from arthritis while working in the garden by following some simple tips.

"Although pain and limited motility can make outdoor work difficult, there are many ways to overcome this," says Dr Arthur Grayzel, senior vice-president for medical affairs of the Arthritis Foundation in America. Here are some of his suggestions:

• Don't kneel on the ground, but sit on a small stool instead, so reducing stress on the joints.

• Use plant containers that are high off the ground – or small raised garden beds – to reduce stretching and bending.

• Don't work for long periods with a tool that you have to grasp firmly.

• Divide your garden into several smaller areas and concentrate on one of these at a time to avoid overdoing things.

• Don't grip heavy loads with your fingers or arms, but carry them in your arms.

• If you have to lift something that

is low or at ground level, be sure to always bend your knees first and do the lifting with a straight back.

• Look in your garden centre for tools specially made for people with arthritis. Alternatively, make your own by putting extension handles on ordinary trowels or weeders. The longer handles will prevent you from having to bend.

• Wash away the pain of arthritis

Many different kinds of arthritic pains will respond speedily to simple water-based treatments, according to Barney Ostrow, top physical therapist at the prestigious Rusk Institute of New University Medical Center, who said: "These therapies can give you better flexibility, reduced swelling and relief from pain."

These are some of his soothing water remedies:

MOIST HEAT REMEDY. Cover the affected area with a dry cotton cloth which can hold the moisture you apply to it with strips of flannel dipped in hot water. Keep the strips over the affected area for about 30 minutes. "This is a very effective way of relieving chronic joint inflammation," Mr. Ostrow said.

HOT WATER MASSAGE. Stand directly under a hot shower and direct a heavy stream onto the aching area for about 20 minutes or so. "Don't use water that's too hot," he added. "It should be just comfortably hot, and when you

finish, cover the area with a piece of warm, dry flannel to prevent chills. It's also a good idea to rub a small amount of baby oil into the skin after each heat application to stop your skin from drying out or becoming chapped."

HEAT LAMP AND HOT WATER REMEDY. Drape hot moist towels over the affected area and shine an infrared heat lamp directly on the cloth. However, you must be extremely careful in handling the lamp's electrical components and, if your hands are wet or moist, be sure to dry them first. Also you should never do this in a bathroom. You also need to ensure that the lamp is placed safely so that it can not fall or be tipped over.

COLD WATER REMEDIES. "For many people, cold water can be extremely soothing because it narrows the blood vessels and induces numbness to ease the pain," Mr. Ostrow explained. Here are some ways that you could use cold, moist applications . . .

• Fill a cut off sleeve from an old garment with crushed ice and apply for 20 to 30 minutes to the affected area. The icy water seeping through the cloth will help ease pain.

• If you don't want to get the affected area wet, you could alternatively put crushed ice cubes in a small plastic bag and rub the bag over the affected area.

• Should you wake in the morning feeling stiff and sluggish, try massaging your body with a coarse bath glove that has been dipped in icy water. For maximum effect, have a warm shower first, and then gradually turn it down to cold and finish with a body rub with the iced glove, Mr. Ostrow advised. "Many of my patients say that this is a very powerful form of pain relief. Just two or three strokes over each aching area should be enough. Dry your body immediately with a coarse bath towel."

• Your hands can give early warning of arthritis

Your hands can provide some early warning signs of incipient arthritis and even indicate the type it might be, according to the experts.

"These signs often appear before you develop any aches or pains," explained Dr Frederick McDuffie, medical director of the American Arthritis Foundation. "Noticing them beforehand – no pun intended – may make it possible to initiate treatment as early as possible."

These are some of the early warnings to look out for:
• Osteoarthritis may be indicated if you have a hard, bony swelling of the middle joint of the fingers or of the joint nearest to the fingernail.
• A swelling, which is both spongy and inflamed, of the knuckles and the middle joint of the fingers might mean rheumatoid arthritis.
• Small pits in the fingernails which leave them looking as though they had been pricked by a pin may

be indicative of psoriatic arthritis.
• So-called 'clubbing' of the fingernails may be a warning sign of hypertrophic pulmonary osteoarthropathy. Usually fingernails slope somewhat down near the base of the nail, but when they are clubbed, there is no dip and the nail is raised and may look swollen.
• A quite hard, bony feeling and swelling of the knuckles where the fingers join the hands could mean haemochromatotic arthritis, which is often caused by too much iron in the body.
• Gouty arthritis – which is caused by too much uric acid in the blood – often first shows itself by small, chalky-white deposits just under the skin and next to the finger joints.
• The gradual disappearance of normal wrinkles from your hands and knuckles can be an early sign of scleroderma, a type of arthritis which makes the skin tighten and is usually accompanied by pain in the joints.

ASPIRIN

• Aspirin works faster with caffeine

You can speed up the action of aspirin if you take caffeine at the same time.

"The combination of the two work sooner at relieving pain," said Dr Bernard Schachtel, a Yale University lecturer in epidemiology, who has just completed a study which tested 207 patients with sore throats by dividing them into three groups. The first group received just aspirin; the second aspirin and caffeine; and the last a placebo.

"Those who had aspirin and caffeine started to get pain relief within 15 minutes, while it took much longer for the effect to work on those who had aspirin alone," he said.

"Although various medications combining aspirin and caffeine are on the market, taking plain aspirin with a cup of strong coffee would work just as well," he added.

• The other side of ASPIRIN

Aspirin could increase the risk of stroke in some people, claims a new study.

According to researchers at the University of Sydney in Australia and the University of Louisville in Kentucky, who studied a total of 242 subjects, people who ordinarily had a lesser risk of suffering a stroke were up to three times more vulnerable if they took aspirin every day with the stroke rate rising from two per cent of the patients to about five per cent.

A small daily dose of aspirin has, of course, been recommended for some time now as a way of preventing heart attacks in cases of unstable angina or following a previous myocardial infarction.

ASTHMA

• Gland operation eases BREATHING

A simple operation can allow asthmatics to breathe more easily, claims a noted chest surgeon who pioneered the controversial procedure.

The surgery – known as 'bilateral carotid body resection' – removes two small glands from each side of the neck and was developed by Dr Benjamin Winter, of West Hollywood Hospital in Los Angeles. Explaining how it works, he said:

"Respiratory diseases destroy only a portion of the lungs and leave a large amount of healthy tissue that is perfectly functional. However, a reflex system that involves the brain, the carotid bodies, the nervous system and the lungs, paralyses that good tissue and makes it useless, causing bronchial tubes to constrict and congest. Removing the carotid bodies breaks that reflex and allows the lungs to open, empty themselves of mucus and altogether work better – although this, of course, won't restore tissue that has already been destroyed."

Dr Winter - who will only operate on patients who don't respond to conventional treatments – says that the results of his procedure are astounding and that some patients who hadn't been able to take a deep breath for years suddenly found that they could even run within a day after surgery.

ASTROLOGY

• Why astrology is good for you

Reading your horoscope can bring you all kinds of surprising benefits, says a psychiatrist who has made a special study of the astrology business.

"Getting advice from fortune-tellers and astrologers can do you a power of good," explained Dr Robert Amstadter, chairman of the department of medicine at Horizon Hospital, Pomona, California. "All of these people typically give you a positive message – telling you that beneficial changes are in the air and encouraging you to behave accordingly.

"And, if you believe in their predictions, you begin to feel better about the world and about yourself. You'll also start to feel more confident and better able to face life's challenges.

"Quite often, the advice is just what someone needs to make an important change as they may have been hemming and hawing, needing just a small push to get going."

BABIES

• Babies can learn sign language

Babies can use sign language by the age of nine months – two or three months sooner than they can usually begin to speak.

A study of homes where sign language is used – usually because one or both parents are deaf or mute – showed that parents formed signs in their infants' hands much as speaking parents encourage their children to repeat words.

"And, it seems that babies can grasp the concept of signing at a much earlier age than they can vocalise words," said one of those involved in the study conducted by scientists at the University of Virginia, Charlottesville, USA. "This finding could have massive implications for our understanding of how babies acquire new skills."

• Babies will be fingerprinted

Police are advising on a scheme to introduce the fingerprinting of newborn babies at Dydley Road Hospital, Birmingham. "Each baby will have its prints taken immediately after birth and this will help prevent mix-ups and abductions," said Judith French, who heads the maternity ward. "Copies of the fingerprint record will be given to the parents so that there can never be any doubt about identifying a baby."

Midwife Josephine Campbell-Kelly got the idea for the scheme when she was given the wrong baby to feed in hospital a few years ago.

American hospitals have been routinely making prints of babies' feet for many years now – the 'footprints' being used instead of fingerprints for the larger surface they provide thereby making comparison easier for non-experts.

• PREMATURE BABIES score low at school

Babies who are born prematurely are up to three times more likely than the average to have difficulties later at school, according to a new study reported in The Lancet medical journal.

The Dutch survey – which analysed the school results achieved by 813 children that had been born prematurely – also found that almost one in five of these was in need of special education by the age of nine.

• Top tips to help turn your baby into a whiz kid

Providing your baby – no matter how young – with the right kind of stimulation will boost his or her intelligence. That's the finding of Dr Susan Luddington-Hoe, director of the Infant Stimulation Education Association of California. "And, it's never too soon to start," she says, "because everything a baby sees, hears, touches, tastes and smells is an experience. I advise all parents to stimulate their babies as much as possible and as soon as possible so as to give them every advantage right from day one."

These are her top tips:

1) Mobiles are still the best toys for very young children. They should, however, be quite close to the baby because up to the age of about one month babies are near-sighted.

2) Adding a few noise-making devices – such as rattles or boxes containing little bells – to the mobile will help stimulate hearing. Be sure that the items are safely attached to the mobile and can't fall down.

3) Provide newborn infants with plenty of opportunities to extend their viewing fields. Babies will make greater use of their eyes when they are sitting upright, so ensure that they spend lots of time on your lap.

4) Now and then move the child's crib or bed so that new views are on offer. Looking at the same parts of a room can become boring.

5) From the age of about two months and older, babies can see quite clearly as far as the ceiling, so make it interesting by safely sticking various designs on it and changing these frequently.

6) Spend as much time as you can with your child. Babies are much more interested in people than in things and this will therefore stimulate their thinking processes.

7) Put stimulating objects within the baby's seeing range. Objects that reflect light – such as mirrors or shiny ornaments – are particularly interesting to newborns.

However, while stimulation is good for developing the baby's senses, you musn't overdo this, adds Dr Luddington-Hoe. When the baby turns away or starts to cry, give it a chance to have a rest.

• When baby doesn't smile

Babies who don't smile or who only do so very infrequently may have an iron deficiency, says Dr Frank Oski, a child care specialist in Syracuse, New York.

Dr Oski added that a week after treatment a previously unhappy-looking, iron-deficient infant usually became a happy baby. Treatment approaches include using breast feeding – if that wasn't done before – or giving the young patient iron fortified formulas. It needs to be pointed out, however, that nothing should be done by parents until after they have checked it out first with their own doctor.

• Widespread myths about babies

Paediatrician Dr Dewey Nemec collects old wives' tales about babies. "Some of them are quite amazing," says the Nashville, Tennessee, USA, doctor. "But many mothers still believe them."

Here are a few of the stranger myths – all of them, of course, quite untrue:
• Tickling an infant's feet will make it stutter.
• If a baby starts to walk at a very early age, it's not because it is making room for other children to be born in the family.
• A baby's hiccups do not mean that it is putting on a sudden spurt of growth.
• Cats left alone with a baby will

not suck its breath out.
• Turning a baby on its tummy will not make it ugly.
• A baby who doesn't fall out of bed during its first year won't grow up to be an adult.

BACKACHE

• Heat sheet stops BACKACHE

A New England doctor has used his Yankee ingenuity to devise a simple, inexpensive and energy efficient way to bring relief to sufferers from backache.

His backache aid consists of a metallised heat-reflecting sheet that's placed between the mattress and the bottom sheet of the bed. "This is an easy and effective way to apply extra heat to the back," said Dr George Bell, a retired cardiologist, of Hyannisport, Mass. "I've found that the sheet works just as well, and sometimes, even better, than elaborate electric heating pads and hot water devices.

"The heat, of course, is free and it's amazing how much of it the human body can generate," he added. "I came up with the idea after suffering from backache myself."

• Super-tight jeans can be a real pain

Wearing jeans that are too tight can give you a real pain in the rear by putting pressure on nerves in the skin between the lower spinal cord and the thigh, says Dr Alois Scharli, of Lucerne, Switzerland.

"The extra pressure caused by the jeans can cause inflammation of the nerves and, in extreme cases, this may need surgical intervention," he warned. "I've seen dozens of cases of teens with inflamed nerves, and all but one had worn tight jeans. One girl even refused to take them off to be examined because she was afraid that she wouldn't be able to get them on again."

BALDNESS

• Hair colour may determine BALDNESS risk

The colour of your hair may indicate how great your risk is of going bald prematurely, according to a survey whose results were reported at a recent meeting of the Society for Investigative Dermatology in the USA.

The study looked at more than 240 patients who had male pattern baldness, ranging in age from 23 to 89. As was expected, baldness was most prevalent in those who were older and also those whose fathers had also been bald. The next most significant factor, however, was colour of hair with men with fair hair, whether blondish or reddish, having experienced much greater loss than those who had black or brown hair.

Commented one expert: "There's possibly a very simple explanation

for this hair-colour link to baldness and that is that it may be because more ultraviolet radiation from the sun gets to the scalps of those who are light haired and this leads to damage to the scalp that results in hair loss. In fact, this is really one more good reason why you should wear a hat."

• The link between baldness and heart risks

Apart from the fact that both are more likely to affect men over a certain age, it had hitherto been assumed that there wasn't any other link between baldness and heart attack.

An American researcher, Dr Peter Baylor, of Houston, now believes that there is a connection between the two conditions and that this lies in a special substance called nitric oxide that's produced by the blood vessel linings and which while acting to reduce blood pressure is also a natural hair growth stimulator. "It follows from that that if the production of nitric oxide is inhibited or impaired, that the patient may have higher blood pressure than normal as well as less vigorous replacement hair growth," he explained, "although it will still take quite a bit more research to definitely establish the link between the two."

BLEPHARITIS

• Sore eyelid cure

Blepharitis, which is an inflammation of the eyelid and usually affects both eyes, is a fairly common problem. Although there are various medications for this condition, this is what the Eye Clinic of the Eastbourne District General Hospital recommends as a simple home treatment for its patients:

• Add one teaspoonful of sodium bicarbonate, BP (which you can get from any pharmacy) to one pint of water that has been fully boiled.
• Mix thoroughly and leave to cool.
• Keep the solution in a clean screw-top jar or bottle with the lid or cap screwed down tight, as that way the treatment will keep for up to four weeks.
• Bathe the eyelid margins with cotton buds or cotton wool soaked in the solution at least twice a day (morning and evening).

Although blepharitis is often a temporary condition, it can also be chronic and bring about outbreaks of styes or ulcers that can result in soreness of the eyes and even impair vision. Therefore, it is essential that you should see your doctor if the condition persists.

BLISTERS

• Grease up to prevent blisters

You can prevent developing blisters on your feet when you're going on a long walk or wearing new shoes that haven't been broken in by greasing up the areas on your feet where blisters are most likely to appear. Use petroleum jelly or any thick ointment to smear the relevant parts.

BLOOD PRESSURE

• Salt may help keep blood pressure DOWN

Contrary to everything that we've all been told, there's now evidence that salt may in fact help keep your blood pressure down rather than increase it.

This startling theory has been put forward by Dr David A. McCarron of the Oregon Hypertension Program at the Oregon Health Sciences University in Portland, USA, where a team of researchers studied more than 10,000 people and found that those subjects using the most salt in their diet had fewer cases of hypertension – that is blood pressure higher than the commonly accepted safe level – than those who hardly took in any salt at all.

"This flies in the face of everything we've been told in the past," said Dr McCarron, adding that "further studies would be needed to confirm the findings and that in the meantime people shouldn't assume that it was safe to start using large amounts of salt again."

The study looked at how 17 different nutrients affected the blood pressure levels of 10,732 subjects, ranging in age from 18 to 74 years, and concluded that the real underlying cause of hypertension appeared to be the lack of four nutrients: calcium, potassium, vitamin A and vitamin C – in the diets of those affected.

The researchers also discovered that the more dairy products were consumed by an individual, the less likely he or she was to be hypertensive. "Calcium seems to be most important in keeping blood pressure levels down and from our assessment we would advise that individuals maintain a calcium intake of at least 800 to 1,000 milligrams a day," added Dr McCarron. "Just four servings a day of dairy products such as milk, yogurt, cheese or even ice cream should be enough to meet the need for these nutrients."

• New salt may reverse HYPERTENSION

A new kind of salt that's low in sodium and contains the minerals magnesium and potassium as well as the amino acid lysine may be able to reverse some of the damaging effects of a high salt diet, such as high blood pressure.

Research recently concluded in Finland indicates that many people with elevated blood pressures suffer from a magnesium deficiency which may keep the usual drug remedies for hypertension from working efficiently.

When the new preparation was used for up to six months on patients with high blood pressure – who had been previously treated

with drugs – it was found that there was a significant drop in pressure. In studies conducted on hypertensive animals, it was also found that those given the new salt lived up 50 to 100 per cent longer than those fed regular table salt.

• Why Your BLOOD PRESSURE reading may be wrong

Your blood pressure reading may be wrong if you hold your arm incorrectly when it is being taken – that's the warning given by Dr Peter W. F. Wilson, director of laboratories for the world famous Framingham Heart Study in the United States.

"Holding your arm in the wrong position – that is either higher or lower than your heart – can cause an error in the readings of as much as ten points for both the upper and lower pressures," he said. "To get the most accurate reading, your arm should be bent at the elbow at a 45-degree angle, with the whole forearm supported on a smooth surface that is level with your heart. If you're lying down when the pressure is taken, there's no problem, but the position of your arm is vitally important if you're sitting or standing."

BLOOD TYPE

• Does your blood match your job?

Japanese researchers claim that they have discovered that people with certain personalities have specific blood types. Now bosses there are basing their hiring policy on the following indicators:

- High achievers – Type O.
- Profound thinkers – Type A.
- Creative people – Type B.
- Good problem-solvers – Type AB.

BLOOD-LETTING

- **Blood-letting makes a comeback**

A modern form of blood-letting, which was an ancient medical remedy for many ailments, is being used for the treatment of some disorders by Dr Kenneth Shumak, of Toronto General Hospital, Ontario, Canada.

The technique – called plasmapheresis – washes impurities from the blood, replaces fluid and recycles the cleansed blood back into the patient. "Physicians once thought they could cure illness by drawing out 'bad' blood," said Dr Shumak. "In fact, George Washington probably died because of this practice. What we're doing is somewhat different because the blood is returned to the patient after purification. The therapy appears to be particularly useful in treating some forms of immune system disorders as well as having applications with multiple sclerosis and rheumatoid arthritis, although these latter uses are still not fully proven scientifically."

BLUSHING

- **Blushing shows you're brainy**

People who blush are showing high intelligence as their cheeks turn pink, according to an expert.

"Blushing starts in the brain, beginning usually with a flicker of embarrassment or a moment of surprise," explained Dr Jonathan Wilkin, a dermatologist at McGuire Veterans Administration Center in Richmond, Virginia, USA. "Yet that tiny emotional derailment fires a signal from the brain to the blood vessels in the face and causes them to become enlarged. This, in turn, stimulates the flow of blood to the face ... and, presto, you're blushing!"

It now seems, although the evidence is not yet conclusive, that the more intelligent you are, the more you're likely to blush. "A possible explanation for this could be that an intelligent, sensitive person will experience embarrassment more easily and more acutely than someone who is less bright," said one researcher.

BODY FAT

- **Why older women have more fat in the winter**

Women who feel that their bodies are flabbier at the beginning of a new year may still put this down to overeating over the holidays. But that's not the reason, say researchers, who have found that it's absolutely natural for older women to become plumper during the winter months.

After studying nearly a hundred women who had gone through the menopause, experts at Tuft Medical School in the United States discovered that both the amount of body fat and how it is distributed in various parts of the body shifts according to the seasons. One particularly noteworthy aspect of this shifting process was that during the winter women carried more fat, especially so in the torso and the legs.

During the study, the amounts of fat, lean and bone tissues on the subjects were carefully measured on three separate occasions six months apart. "Overall, the women's weight didn't actually change," reported one researcher. "But as a group the women were found to have considerably more lean tissue during the summer months – and a good deal more fat in the winter."

BOREDOM

• Bored into illness

Being bored can actually make you sick. That's the claim of Dr Augustin de la Pena, a researcher with the Center for Sleep Disorders in San Jose, California. "The human brain will do almost anything for the sake of stimulation and challenge," he said, "and that includes undermining the mind of its owner as the bored brain begins to entertain itself by producing illness."

Dr de la Pena, who has conducted numerous studies on boredom's effects, noted that scientific literature abounded with examples of people who suffered mental disorders when they had nothing to do. "When you're bored, your body's production of prostaglandins increases and this acts to intensify pain," he added. "So a bad back that troubles you but little when you're busy suddenly becomes truly painful when you're bored.

"More evidence of the deteriorating effect of boredom can be found in the high illness and mortality rates of newly retired people who, when they have little to do, often experience a rapid decline in health."

BOWEL CANCER

• Beat BOWEL CANCER with aspirin

Taking a daily aspirin can reduce the risk of bowel cancer, which is the second most common killer cancer in Britain, according to a recent study completed at the University of Nottingham.

Researchers found that patients who used the drug regularly had halved their risk of developing growths that could eventually lead to bowel cancer.

BREAKFAST

• Breakfast is good for your brain

We were always told that a hearty breakfast was good for us. Now a British doctor has finally proven it.

Dr David Benton compared the performances of two sets of university students who sat tests. One group had had a strong glucose drink to start the day while the other had to make do with a 'placebo' drink which had no nutritional content.

"Those who had taken the glucose had much faster recall than those who had nothing," he reported. "The message from this is very clear: people who have higher blood glucose have better memories."

BREAST CANCER

• Foods that cut BREAST CANCER risk

Eating a diet that's rich in fruits and vegetables may help lower the chances of breast cancer in pre-menopausal women.

Six hundred and twenty-six women were interviewed by Dr Jo Freudenheim, professor of social and preventive medicine at the State University of New York at Buffalo. Of these, 310 were pre-menopausal women, aged over 40 years, who had been affected by breast cancer. The other 316 women had been randomly selected from the general population and matched the ages of the first group, the one important difference being that they had not had cancer.

"The results showed that the women from the control group – that is those who did not have cancer – ate considerably more fruit and vegetables than those who had the disease," reported Dr Freudenheim. "This finding is highly encouraging because it may help us understand new ways of preventing breast cancer."

• Go on war diet to beat breast cancer

Today's schoolgirls would be well advised to go on a diet similar to that forced upon youngsters by wartime rationing in the early 1940s because that would probably substantially reduce their future risk of breast cancer, says one of Britain's top experts on the disease.

The recommendation followed the recent discovery that the rate of breast cancer had been cut for a whole generation of women with the number of victims aged between 45 and 55 years of the disease showing a 10 per cent drop in Scotland.

"This drop is among women who were born during, before, and after the war and who are now at an age when they are getting breast cancer," said Professor Gordon McVie, scientific director of the

Cancer Research Campaign. "The figures are considerably lower than expected or predicted."

Professor McVie thought that the drop was the result of the women's diet in their early years when they ate very little meat, sugar or dairy products, but were given orange juice and cod liver oil every day to provide vitamins A, C and D. "The wartime diet was brilliant," he said. "And, here is the first evidence of a protective diet in young girls paying off later by reducing breast cancer."

Although Professor McVie accepted that it was difficult for today's mothers to control their children's diet because they had easy access to sweets and junk foods, he added, "the least mothers should be doing is checking that their children's vitamin intake from fruit and vegetables is enough."

Britain has one of the world's worst records for breast cancer with 26,000 new cases being reported and 15,000 women dying from the disease each year.

• Hormone pill may treat BREAST CANCER

A massive trial currently underway at London's Royal Marsden Hospital hopes to find not only a way of treating breast cancer with a hormone pill, but of also establishing a way to identify those who are most at risk from the deadly disease.

Two thousand women – all of them apparently healthy, but considered to be at high risk because of a family history of breast cancer –

have been recruited into the trial which aims to identify the gene responsible and discover how it is passed on in families. "Prevention studies are crucial," said specialist Dr Trevor Powles, who heads the project.

At the same time, Dr Powles is also conducting a national trial of 'tamoxifen', a hormone pill that has been claimed to be effective in treating cancer. "I feel that of all possible interventions that could be used, tamoxifen is likely to be the safest, the only realistic option in the foreseeable future," he stated.

BREAST-FEEDING

• Extra vitamin D for babies the natural way

Nursing mothers can dramatically increase the vitamin D content of their breast milk by the simple expedient of sunbathing for just half an hour a day, according to a study by the Wisconsin Perinatal Center in Madison.

During tests conducted on nursing mothers, the concentration of vitamin D in their milk rose sharply after they had been exposed to sunshine for 30 minutes. And the levels remained higher for up to two weeks thereafter.

"This effect could be critical for the growing number of breast-fed babies who depend on their mother's milk as a source of vitamin D, which, of course, is vital in warding off rickets," said one of the researchers.

• Now Daddy can breast-feed, too

Fathers can now breast-feed their babies almost like mothers thanks to a new device.

Developed by Dr Alfred Goldson, chairman of radiation therapy at Howard University in Washington, the device is a bib that the father slips around his neck and which provides two openings at breast level where a bottle can be inserted. Although the bottle-laden bib hardly looks like real breasts, it's just as efficient at getting the job done as far as the baby is concerned.

Dr Goldson created the 'Baby Bonder' bib after his wife argued that he would never be as close to their baby as she because he lacked breasts to feed it.

BREATH

• What your breath can tell your doctor

A chemical analysis of your breath will soon enable doctors to quickly and painlessly diagnose a wide variety of illnesses, say researchers at Loyola University in Chicago, USA.

The breath analyser has so far proven itself as being effective in diagnosing rheumatoid arthritis, multiple sclerosis, heart attacks, and may even be useful in helping surgeons determine when a patient who had a heart transplant may be rejecting the new organ. "This last application is, of course, of paramount importance to transplant surgery," explained one of the researchers. "And, it's particularly valuable because the breath analysis detects the slightest rejection and does so much sooner than other methods."

"The way the breath analyser works is by detecting minute amounts of a chemical compound called pentane which results from the destruction of cell membranes associated with all of the above conditions," he added.

Although the role of pentane has been known to medical science for a long time, it is only recently that equipment has become sophisticated enough to detect its levels from a patient's single breath.

It is expected that the new diagnostic tool will also be extremely useful in dealing with potential heart attack victims as the breath analyser takes only about 20 minutes to produce its results, much quicker than current blood analysis.

BRUISING

• No more black and blue marks

You can prevent black and blue marks from appearing if, as soon as you've bruised yourself, you wet your fingers and dip them into granulated white sugar. Rigorously massage the affected area with your sugar-coated fingers, ensuring that you reach somewhat beyond the bruising. This treatment will help reduce the area of broken capillaries and thereby lessen the chance of a black and blue mark forming.

BURNS

• The honey cure for oil splatters

It's happened to all of us who wield a frying pan – those quite irritating oil splatters that jump out of the pan onto our hands and create minor burns. Here's a tried and tested traditional remedy that takes the sting out of minor oil splatter burns: spread a light layer of honey over the burns. Honey is a rich source of healing enzymes and will also make the sting disappear within minutes.

CALORIES

• Want to burn calories? Get high

If you get high enough – that's high in altitude, not on drink – you'll burn calories faster.

That is the finding of nutritional biochemist, Robert Reynolds, who studied the number of calories burned by members of an expedition team that climbed Mount Everest. One climber burned an astounding 8,000 calories a day while others at the base camp, located at 17,500 feet, consumed nearly 3,300 calories, just about the same as a marathon runner does during a race.

"I believe that the thin air at high altitudes, which only contains about half the oxygen as that at sea level, is the reason why calories are burned up at such a fantastic rate," said the researcher. "However, you have to be at an altitude of more than 15,000 feet before the effect starts to work."

• Not all calories are equal

With slimming diets all being based on calorie counts, you might be forgiven for believing that a calorie is a calorie, no matter whether it comes from a slice of bread or the butter you spread on it.

"That view is quite wrong," asserts Dr Jean-Pierre Flatt, of the University of Massachusetts Medical School. "Calories from dietary fat – such as butter – are more fattening than those from carbohydrates – such as bread – because fat requires less energy to be converted from food to body fat. Although nearly a quarter of the calories taken in as carbohydrates are burned off in the food-to-fat conversion, less than one in thirty of fat calories are consumed the same way."

This view is backed up by evidence from studies conducted by Dr Elliott Danforth at the University of Vermont where men who were overfed on a diet rich in carbohydrates took seven months to gain 30 pounds. On the other hand, men overfed by somewhat fewer calories – but as part of a diet rich in fat – gained the same amount of weight in only three months, less than half the time of the first group. Added Dr Danforth: "There's no question that fat is more fattening, calorie for calorie, than carbohydrates."

• How much jogging burns off a soft drink?

Ever been tempted to cheat on your diet, telling yourself that you'll make up for it by taking some extra exercise?

Well, this is how long you'd have to exercise to burn up the calories contained in the snacks listed below:
• A four-ounce serving of ice cream (average 150 calories): 43 minutes of walking; 12 of bicycling; or 11 of jogging.
• A slice of pizza (245 calories): 70 minutes walking; 22 bicycling; or 18 jogging.
• Ten potato chips (110 calories): 31 minutes walking; 10 bicycling; or 8 jogging. And, an eight-ounce normal cola drink (105 calories) would require just about the same amount of exercise.

CANCER

• Fight CANCER with carrots

Eating a couple of carrots a day could well be the answer to keeping certain cancers at bay, according to scientists who have been studying the wonder vegetable.

Carrots, of course, are noted for being a rich source of beta-carotene, a substance that produces a particularly potent form of vitamin A that doctors believe may help in preventing cancer by reducing the genetic damage in cells which is believed to set the stage for cancer. In one recent study, beta-carotene was found to dramatically reduce the number of damaged cells in patients with a high risk of contracting mouth or lip cancer.

"It cut the the number of genetically damaged cells which we believe are pre-cancerous – by 400 per cent," explained Dr Richard San, who headed the study conducted at the University of British Columbia, in Vancouver, Canada. These findings suggest that if you get enough anti-cancer agents, such as beta-carotene, you're in a better position to fight off many of the cancer causing agents you're exposed to.

• Common mineral cuts cancer risk

A study recently completed in Finland has discovered that men who had lower than average levels of selenium in their blood were much more likely to contract cancer, particularly of the stomach and pancreas.

"We studied 39,268 men and women and found that the average selenium level for males with cancer was significantly lower than in those who didn't have the disease," reported Dr Paul Knekt, a public health physician at the Social Insurance Institution in Helsinki. "For all types of cancer, we found that men afflicted by it had 5.8 per cent less selenium in their blood than those who were cancer-free."

The link between low selenium and cancer incidence was even more marked for certain specific types of the disease. "For example, those men without cancer had 10.8 per cent greater selenium levels than male patients with stomach cancer," added Dr Knekt. "And, men in the study who were free of the disease had a staggering 19.6 per cent higher selenium levels than those with pancreatic cancer."

Commenting on these results, Dr Gerhard Schrauser, professor of chemistry at the University of California in San Diego, said: "Without a doubt, selenium reduces the risks of all types of cancer."

The Finnish study wasn't the first to note the correlation between low selenium and cancer as similar surveys in Japan, Israel and China has also concluded that the mineral reduced cancer incidence.

Although these findings would seem to indicate that it would be advisable to increase your selenium intake, another expert cautioned that people shouldn't overdo this. "Taking up to 70 micrograms of selenium is safe," said Dr Larry Clark, professor of epidemiology at the University of Arizona. "That's the government's recommended daily allowance. Although selenium is available as supplements, be careful not to take too much."

Rich natural sources of selenium include eggs, all seafoods, meat, grain products and garlic.

• How skimmed milk cuts CANCER RISK

Drinking low-fat or skimmed milk can substantially decrease your risk of getting cancer, according to a recent study. The milk-drinking habits of more than 4,600 subjects were recorded in a massive survey at the Roswell Park Memorial Institute, a world-renowned cancer research centre in the United States, and the results showed that:

• People who drink low-fat milk have a much smaller chance of contracting many different kinds of cancer than those who drink whole milk or no milk.

• The risk factor is lowered even further for those who choose skimmed milk instead of low-fat milk.

• The low-fat and skimmed milk appeared to provide particular protection against the following common cancers: rectal, lung, cervical, oral and stomach cancer.

"I believe that low-fat or skimmed milk are so effective in lowering the risk of cancer because whole milk contains much more fat, a substance that has been linked to cancer in other studies," explained Dr Curtis Mettlin, who headed the study.

"Low-fat milk contains only one quarter of the fat of whole milk and skimmed milk has about half the fat of low-fat milk."

And, because the cancer risk is about the same for people who drink whole milk or no milk, it would appear that milk does contain certain anti-cancer agents but that these may be cancelled out when there's also a high fat content. In other words, milk in itself is likely to be helpful in preventing cancer, providing you don't take in too much fat at the same time.

• Fish oil may hold clue to cancer cure

Scientists at Birmingham's Aston University have identified the protein that raids the body's fat reserves to feed cancer cells and have found that they can attack this protein with a highly purified oil extracted from salmon, sardines and mackerel.

"Clinical trials are to start soon and it is hoped that the new treatment may be available within two years for patients with lung, stomach or pancreas cancer," said Professor Michael Tisdale, who led the pioneering research which was initiated after he noticed that some cancers stopped sufferers from absorbing food properly.

"We have been looking for a link between diet and cancer for 20 years now and this could be it," said Professor Gordon McVie, scientific director of the Cancer Research Campaign. "This discovery brings all the pieces together as there has been a lot of evidence that people who eat a lot of fish have fewer instances of cancer."

• It's official – the pill protects against certain CANCERS

A leading British expert has stated that there is now definite proof that the oral contraceptive pill protects women against cancer of the ovaries or womb as well as having a protective role in certain menstrual, breast and pelvic problems.

"More research is, however, still needed to fully assess if women over the age of 35 face a higher risk of breast cancer if they're taking the pill," said Professor Martin Vessey, head of Oxford University's department of public health and primary care. "The benefits of the contraceptive pill for women in that age group may have to be reassessed if major breast cancer studies currently being carried out in Britain and the Netherlands find them to be at increased risk."

In the past, some research on the older high dosage pills had suggested they could possibly have adversely affected the rate of heart attacks and strokes.

• Vitamin A compound can block CANCER

A form of vitamin A – which hitherto had been primarily used in reducing wrinkles – has been found to have remarkable powers to block the development of certain cancers.

The cancer fighting ability of the compound 13-cis retinoic acid was discovered during a study conducted by Dr Scott Lippman, assistant professor of medicine at the University of Texas, when it successfully halted the further development of head, neck and mouth cancers.

One part of the study concentrated on 100 patients who had pre-cancerous head and neck lesions. Forty-nine of them were given retinoic acid and only three of these went on to develop tumours. Out of the other 51 – who were treated with different compounds – 14 developed tumours.

And, the lesions only became worse in 2 patients out of 24 with pre-cancerous mouth lesions who received retinoic acid, as compared with 16 out of 29 similar cases becoming worse while being treated with a different compound.

• Taking the pain out of CANCER screenings

Mammograms are a vital part of cancer prevention but the procedure can be so painful that many women simply refuse to return for further screenings.

But the pain associated with mammograms may soon be at an end thanks to an ingenious new device invented by Dr Phyllis Kornguth, chief of the breast imaging section at Duke University in America.

During mammography, the woman's breasts are squeezed between an X-ray plate and a compression paddle. The squeezing is necessary to ensure a clear image on the film, but when the pressure – which is normally controlled by a technician – is too high, the pain for the woman can be excruciating.

Dr Kornguth's solution was as simple as it was obvious: let the woman herself control the degree of pressure applied by the compression paddle. To test this idea she had an engineer fit her department's mammography machines with a small handheld control button which the subject could use to regulate the pressure. "It worked wonders during a test series," she said. "Virtually every woman preferred to control the pressure herself and the patients have been much more willing to come back for regular mammograms."

The control button can be added easily and cheaply to "any mammographic devices," she added.

CARPAL TUNNEL SYNDROME

• Laser treats hand pain and swelling

A new kind of non-surgical laser is being used to treat carpal tunnel syndrome and is getting much better results than the traditional methods of treatment which usually involve wrist splints, drugs, or even surgery.

"We've used the new laser on 300 patients so far and nearly 90 per cent of them have regained total use of their hands and are free of pain," reported Dr Chad Smith, clinical professor of orthopaedic surgery at the University of Southern California.

During treatment, the doctor holds the laser against the patient's wrist for three half-minute bursts during which the invisible light penetrates the skin, reducing painful swelling and increasing blood flow. The procedure is usually repeated every second day for up to five weeks.

Carpal tunnel syndrome – which mainly affects people whose jobs demand repetitive hand motions, like typists, computer operators, and workers on assembly lines – results from the compression of the median nerve as it enters the palm of the hand. This causes pain – which can be very severe – and numbness in the index and middle fingers as well as weakness of the thumb.

CARROTS

- ### Why carrots are good for you

Researchers at Harvard have endorsed what your mother probably told you: "Eat up all your carrots, they're good for you."

A five-year study has conclusively proven that beta-carotene – a special form of vitamin A found not only in carrots, but in many other vegetables and fruits – can significantly cut the risk of heart attack and stroke in patients who already have heart disease.

"We found there was a reduction of more than 50 per cent in heart attack, stroke and cardiovascular death for those patients with existing heart conditions who took a 50-milligram beta-carotene supplement every second day," reported Dr J. Michael Gaziano, cardiology fellow at Harvard's Brigham and Women's Hospital.

"This provides a compelling argument for people to include foods rich in beta-carotene as part of a balanced diet.

"For people with angina or coronary by-pass history, beta-carotene therapy may lessen the likelihood of future major coronary tragedy," he added.

Apart from carrots, other rich sources of beta-carotene include spinach, romaine lettuce, Brussels sprouts, tomatoes, apricots and cantaloupes.

CEREALS

- ### Cereals can be bad for you

You may think that having a bowl of muesli for breakfast is a healthy way to start the day. Not necessarily so, according to a recent report, because the muesli may contain as much fat as two fried eggs and four teaspoonfuls of sugar.

Which? Way to Health magazine reported the following findings recently:

• Richest in fibre were the following breakfast cereals: Nestlé Shredded Wheat, and Sainsbury's Mini Wheats.

• Poorest in fibre were frosted flakes and honey or crunch nut flakes.

• Containing the most fat: Quaker's Tropical Harvest Crunch.

"Cereals can be healthy, but the nutritional value depends on the one you pick," said editor David Dickinson.

CHAPPED HANDS

• Two ways to treat chapped hands

Chapped hands with dry and irritated skin are usually the result of a combination of low humidity and lack of skin oils. Here are two simple home remedies that could help:

1) Soak your hands in warm but not too hot water for about ten minutes. Gently pat off the excess moisture with a clean towel. Apply a very small amount of ordinary vegetable cooking oil or mineral oil. Rub the oil well in so that it becomes absorbed by the skin.

2) If the above doesn't do the trick, try moistening the inside of a pair of cotton gloves with a small amount of petroleum jelly. Wear the gloves in bed overnight so that the jelly can gradually re-moisten tissues. Repeat now and then as needed.

CHILDREN

• Nuts tame schoolchildren

Nuts and raisins make young pupils easier to get along with even if it doesn't improve their grades, report school officials in Madera, California, USA.

A study – called Project Nibble – showed that 200 children in grades two to six who received a mid-morning snack of raisins and nuts had a better attitude towards their teachers and school in general than 200 other students who were not given the snack.

• Orange juice helps children behave

Adding two glasses of orange juice to the diet of youngsters in a juvenile detention centre slashed their disruptive behaviour nearly in half, according to noted American sociologist Stephen Schoenthaler, who is coordinator of criminal justice studies for California State College at Turlock.

The youths, whose average age was 15.4 years, were observed for six months and then the juice was added to their diets for another six months.

"Comparing the incidence of bad

behaviour for the two periods, we found that it was cut almost in half when we supplied the juice," reported Mr Schoenthaler. "We suspect that the orange juice worked so well because it provided extra nutrition which somehow made the kids less aggressive or hostile. Taking this one step further, the best evidence to date suggests that the average family might be wise to make sure that their children have a large glass of orange juice once or twice a day."

• **Don't pity
the only child**

Children without brothers or sisters are more to be envied than pitied – that's the claim of Dr Toni Falbo, a psychologist at the University of Texas in Austin.

Shattering many widely held myths about 'only children', Dr Falbo said: "These kids are usually better off than youngsters who have siblings and they usually aren't lonely, selfish or maladjusted.

"The 'only children' aren't lonely because they often have the same number of friends as other youngsters," added Dr Falbo. "Having to adjust to the same social situations at school and at home, means that the odds on them becoming either selfish or maladjusted are neither greater nor smaller than for other children.

"In fact, 'only children' have some advantages in their favour," he added. "They are often closer to their parents and frequently become better parents themselves. What's more, as a group, they're also better educated and usually end up earning more money and making more rapid advancement in their careers."

CHOLESTEROL

• **Walking lowers
CHOLESTEROL level**

If you walk for at least two and a half hours a week, you'll be less likely to have a high cholesterol level, according to a ground-breaking new survey, the first to show that even very moderate exercise can make a significant contribution to reducing heart disease risk.

More than 3,600 workers were studied during the survey and it was found that those who walked two and a half hours or more every week were 50 per cent less likely to have high cholesterol levels than those who did no exercise.

The walkers were also found to have substantially higher levels of those cholesterol components which are most helpful in avoiding heart disease.

"There's no doubt any more that walking is a healthful thing to do," commented Larry Tucker, Ph.D., one of the co-authors of the study conducted at Brigham Young University in America. "Not only does it reduce cholesterol, but it also improves bone density, controls weight and strengthens the overall cardiovascular system."

• Grape juice can cut CHOLESTEROL levels

Just drinking one glass of grape juice every day may be enough to keep your cholesterol levels in check, say researchers at Cornell University in the United States.

The key to the cholesterol-lowering effect lies in a chemical known as resveratrol that the grape produces naturally to fight off fungal disease. This chemical is, however, lacking in grapes grown for table use because the growers already treat the fruit to protect it from the disease and therefore there is no need for it to manufacture its own defences.

Another source of resveratrol is red wine which Californian authorities have officially endorsed as being capable of reducing heart disease risk.

• To test or not to test?

The value of do-it-yourself kits to test your own cholesterol which have now been available for some months have been questioned by one of Britain's top heart specialists.

"Knowing your own cholesterol level can turn healthy individuals into worried patients," said Professor Larry Ramsay, of the Royal Hallamshire Hospital, Sheffield, who also said that low-fat diets don't necessarily reduce blood cholesterol. "Many of these diets, which are often recommended by family doctors, have little impact on blood fats which are believed to contribute to heart disease," he added. "What's more, keeping to these diets can also cause stress for individuals and their families."

Further doubt about the DIY kits were raised in an article in The Lancet, Britain's leading medical journal, which claimed that cholesterol testing was more effective when done by experienced people who could interpret the results correctly, and that the kits were often difficult to use.

• It's not so bad to be fat – if you're a woman!

Startling new evidence from a massive survey suggests that there is little point in women reducing their cholesterol levels because although this results in a reduction in deaths from heart attacks, this gain is balanced by a similar increase in deaths from other causes.

In most Western countries, including Britain and America, both men and women are advised to eat less fat, less saturated fat and less cholesterol to avoid heart disease. Now a 15-year study of 15,000 adults in Scotland has shown that although women are more likely to have cholesterol levels that are higher than those of men, they are still much less at risk from cardiac problems. The difference between the two sexes is so marked that even the women with the highest level of cholesterol were still less likely to have heart attacks than the men with the lowest levels.

Commented Dr Christopher Isles, of the Dumphries and Galloway Royal Infirmary, who headed the survey: "Most studies have focused on men, the assumption being that such data can be extrapolated for women. There is, however, little evidence to support that belief."

Summing up the findings, he suggested that while low-fat diets were good for men, the best advice for women was to have regular exercise, eat plenty of fruit and vegetables, as well as food containing fat and oils.

Dr Isles's recommendations were endorsed by Ann Walker, senior lecturer in nutrition and food science at Reading University, who said: "Women need to enjoy sensible amounts of a variety of foods on a regular basis. Dietary advice should focus on eating for overall health."

CHRONIC PAIN

- ### Simple diet brings fast relief for chronic pain

You can substantially reduce – or even completely eliminate many kinds of chronic pain with a special diet that's rich in certain carbohydrates and low in fats, protein and sugar, according to the experts.

"This astonishing pain relief diet really works – there's no question about it," declared Dr Samuel Seltzer, a noted pain control expert at Temple University in Philadelphia. "Patients following it have had tremendous success in relieving chronic pains of the head and the neck, such as migraines, headaches and facial neuralgias."

These are the main points of his pain-reducing diet:

- Substantially increase your consumption of complex carbohydrates – these include foods such as wholegrains (with the exclusion of corn), beans vegetables and fruits – so that these make up 70 to 80 per cent of your food intake.
- Avoid refined carbohydrates, such as sugar, honey, and syrups, and cut your total sugar intake by at least 40 per cent.
- Avoid all fats and oils, including butter, margarine, meat fats and lard, as much as possible. Also avoid fatty meats, whole milk, cheese with more than a one per cent fat content, and egg yolks.
- Reduce or eliminate your intake of prepared foods that contain fats, oils, sugar or eggs.
- Give both caffeine and alcohol a miss.

Additionally, Dr Seltzer recommends that you should take a total of three grams of tryptophan – an essential amino acid supplement available in health food shops – every day, dividing this into six equal doses. Tryptophan is converted by the body into serotonin, a pain relieving chemical. Usually the tryptophan dosage can be reduced after the first few weeks and most patients eventually only need a maintenance dose of half a gram a day.

The combination of the special diet and the tryptophan "dramatically elevates your pain tolerance and you can stand pain much better than you would normally," said Dr Seltzer. "The diet also brings results very quickly – in some people it works within a week, while in others it takes only four to six weeks."

The diet plus tryptophan regime is also enthusiastically endorsed by Dr Carol A. Warfield, director of the pain management unit at Beth Israel Hospital in Boston, who said: "It is an effective and safe nutritional approach to pain relief."

Both experts stress that anyone wanting to try the diet should first consult their own doctor.

• Cure chronic pain with a bowl of chilli?

Scientists have discovered that scorchingly hot chilli could contain a natural painkiller.

Tests on animals have shown that capsaicin – the chemical that gives chilli peppers their fiery kick – effectively relieves many types of pain, particularly long-term tumour pain and that caused by pinched nerves.

And, this is how capsaicin works, according to Dr Thomas F. Burks, a pharmacologist at the University of Arizona's Health Sciences Center in Tucson: "It is known that if you press your finger against a hot iron or prick it on a rosebush, a chemical called 'substance P' is released and carries a pain message to the brain.

"What we have discovered is that after treatment with capsaicin, the nerve does not manufacture substance P. So when the nerve is activated it will release the substance P it may have stored up, but – and this is the important part – it doesn't replace it by making more. And, as the nerve runs out of the substance it uses as a neurotransmitter, the link between the site of the pain and the brain is then absent."

Dr Burks emphasised that the answer to pain wasn't simply to gorge yourself on bowls of red-hot chilli as capsaicin was too toxic to ingest enough to affect the whole system. "But chronic pain is localised – it comes from one place," he added. "And, this led us to wonder what would happen if we used it locally . . .

"We put some in the footpad of a guinea pig, in very small doses in the skin, and the guinea pig didn't like that at all. So we mixed the capsaicin with a local anaesthetic called etidocaine and injected that mixture locally in other guinea pigs. By the time the etidocaine had worn off, the capsaicin had become activated.

We then used various techniques to provoke pain and the animals felt nothing . . . and the effects have been lasting for up to ten weeks."

Dr Burks added that the amount of pain that capsaicin would produce when first applied without an anaesthetic varied according to the dosage and compared it to eating hot peppers. "You eat a hot pepper and you get the warmth; you eat a lot of hot peppers and you get the pain," he said.

In a scientific paper submitted to the prestigious journal, Anesthesiology, Dr Burks reported: "Capsaicin produces a long-lasting regional analgesia. Its use in chronic pain deserves extensive study." Now he and his team have applied to the US Food and Drug Administration for permission to conduct experiments with capsaicin on humans.

COFFEE

- ### Anxious, hostile, and depressed?
  ### It could be the coffee!

Coffee's well-known pick-me-up effect may leave you down in the dumps once the brief caffeine high has worn off, warn two scientists.

"Caffeine can make people feel anxious, hostile and depressed," reported Dr Donald Templer and Dr David Veleber, of the California School of Professional Psychology, who examined the brew's effects on 157 men and women.

During the study, one third of the group received no caffeine; another third had a cup and a half of coffee; and the last group drank three cups. One hour later, all participants were tested to find out how their moods had been affected.

On all three parameters which were measured – anxiety, depression, and hostility – the groups who had drunk coffee had the greatest problems.

On the depression scale, the no-coffee group scored only one point - which meant they weren't depressed at all – while the middle group scored six points and the high caffeine group recorded 18 points indicating a high level of feeling low.

The anxiety scale average scores were: no-coffee group, 5 points; middle group, 25; and 27 points for the top group.

On the hostility test, the group that had no coffee scored only 1; the middle group 14; and the high-coffee group 19.

"Although we already knew that coffee could make people anxious, we were surprised to learn that it brought on depression as well," commented the researchers.

- ### Coffee cures
  ### post-lunch dip

There's nothing like a strong cup of coffee to stop you from flagging after lunch, according to a British psychologist.

"The midday meal hits concentration and makes people sluggish," Dr Andrew Smith told experts at the recent conference of the British Psychological Society. "Coffee can counteract and cancel the post-lunch dip. Mostly caffeine consumption is good news rather than bad news."

Dr Smith studied more than 700 people over six years to arrive at his findings, which included:

• The post-lunch dip in concentration began some 45 minutes after eating.

• The ability to concentrate was affected for up to two and a half hours.

• The level of concentration fell by up to 15 per cent.

• Thanks to caffeine, it's a boy!

A couple stands a much better chance of conceiving a boy if the man drinks strong coffee before lovemaking – that's the claim of a leading scientist.

"Drinking a couple of cups of very strong caffeinated coffee some 15 to 30 minutes before intercourse can have a stimulating effect on male-producing sperm and impart some extra speed to it," said Dr Landrum Shettles, co-author with David Rorvik of 'How To Choose The Sex Of Your Baby', published by Doubleday in America. "However, it won't make any difference if the wife drinks the coffee – it must be the husband."

• Drink coffee to keep dentist away

Coffee is so often blamed for being a contributory factor to various health problems that it is refreshing to learn that it may actually help you keep your teeth.

A new study recently completed in America says that the tannin, which is a natural chemical, found in coffee will help prevent plaque-causing bacteria from sticking to your teeth, thereby reducing the chances of developing cavities or gum disease. And, it's not just coffee that provides tannin: other rich sources include tea, beer, wine, and bananas.

COLDS

• Women suffer more from colds

Women get the same number of colds than men, but they suffer more from them, a recent study shows.

The results of a poll of 300 men and women by the pharmaceutical firm SmithKline Beecham revealed:

• The average man or woman catches 2.2 colds a year.

• Women usually say that they caught their colds because of external causes, such as the weather or from other people with colds.

• Men, on the other hand, tend to blame themselves for the colds – such as not getting enough sleep, not taking extra vitamins, or not exercising sufficiently.

• Women are greater believers in the efficacy of over-the-counter medicines.

• And, as a group, women feel more miserable when they have a cold than men do.

• On one point, the two sexes felt the same: both men and women agreed that they wished their spouses would be nicer and more sympathetic to them when they were suffering from a cold.

• Beer can ease COMMON COLD symptoms

There's a great new way to deal with the troublesome symptoms of the common cold – have a few glasses of beer!

According to recent research, coughs, sniffles and sore throats can all respond magically to alcohol.

"Naturally, you musn't overdo this," commented psychologist Andrew Smith, who outlined the study's findings at a recent London conference. "Because if you do, you'll feel a lot worse in the morning than if you had just suffered the cold."

Research conducted with the help of 500 willing volunteers showed that while alcohol didn't stop people from becoming infected with the cold virus, it did substantially reduce the infection's unpleasant symptoms by acting as an anti-inflammatory, he said. Other experts believe that alcohol may also help you avoid catching a cold by its effect in lowering stress, as it's well-known that infections of the upper respiratory tract are much more likely to strike when you're worn out or upset.

The alcohol 'cure' works with any kind of alcoholic beverages and the recommended daily dosage is about one and half pints of beer or three glasses of wine to provide the maximum benefit.

• Don't let your cold play ping-pong

If you have a cold or the flu, it's not unusual for you to infect other members of your family. And, as you're recovering, you may get the symptoms back once again as your nearest and dearest return the original infection to you.

"This method of transmission is called viral ping-pong and it's common in all kinds of households," said Dr Sidney Friedlaender, clinical professor of medicine at the University of Florida School of Medicine, adding that adhering to the following simple procedures would reduce the chances of a cold or flu being spread to others in the family:

• Use only disposable tissues for blowing your nose or when coughing or sneezing. Dispose of used tissues either by burning or sealing them into a plastic bag before putting them into the refuse.

• Have your own towel and wash-cloth or sponge and don't keep these in a bathroom which is in common use when you don't need them.

• Use liquid soap instead of a bar which can hold viral particles.

• Avoid touching other people. Viruses can be spread by simple hand contact.

• Keep a set of plates, glasses and dining utensils for your use only and wash these in very hot, soapy water every time after use.

• Where you just can't catch a COLD

There's a place where it's impossible for you to catch a cold or the flu. The snag is that this paradise is the North Pole in the winter because the temperature there drops so low that the organisms that cause disease just can't survive.

• Prevent COLDS with yogurt

Eating yogurt can help prevent colds and allergy symptoms, according to a study completed at the University of California, where researchers found that people who ate a daily small bowl of active-culture yogurt had one quarter fewer colds than those who didn't.

The study also discovered that allergy sufferers who regularly ate yogurt suffered symptoms for only three days yearly on the average as compared to an 18-day average for others. Summing up the study, Dr Georges Halpern, adjunct professor of medicine at the University's

School of Medicine, said: "If you continually eat at least two small bowls of yogurt daily, you may stave off colds and other upper respiratory infections because your immune system will be enhanced by the active culture that converts milk into yogurt."

COLON CANCER

• How to halve COLON CANCER risk

Taking aspirin regularly may make you up to 50 per cent less likely to develop colon or rectal cancer.

A massive study of 6,217 people conducted at four major medical institutions in the United States revealed that people who took aspirin at least four times a week had half the risk of developing colorectal cancer when compared with others who never took aspirin, or those who used it only occasionally.

Explaining the findings, Dr Paul Stolley, professor of medicine at the University of Pennsylvania School of Medicine, said: "It seems that aspirin may inhibit the formation of substances in the body called prostaglandins which are known to play a role in the growth of tumours."

Added Dr William Castell, an expert in preventive medicine at Harvard Medical School and director of the famed Framingham Heart Study: "Taking aspirin four times a week would not only help reduce the risk of large bowel cancer, but also reduce the risk of heart attacks and heart diseases."

A word of caution, however, before you rush off to buy aspirin: before taking it regularly as a preventive measure you should check first with your own doctor as there are instances where this could be harmful to you.

• The risk of being desk-bound

Men who spend most of their working day sitting behind a desk have a much higher risk of developing colon cancer than those whose jobs require more strenuous physical activity – that's the conclusion reached at the end of special study of the illness.

"Knowing about this link could lead to prevention of the disease by encouraging the desk-bound to take up suitable exercises," said Dr David Garabrant, a specialist in preventive medicine at the University of California in Los Angeles.

COLOUR

• How others react to the colour of your clothes

The colours of your clothes can influence the moods of the people around you – and also affect how they react to you as a person – claims a top psychologist who has made a special study of the subject.

The colour effect essentially comes in two parts: the extent to which a colour pleases the onlooker; and whether or not it is also stimulating, explained Albert Mehrabian, professor of psychology at the University of California in Los Angeles.

According to his findings, the most-pleasing to least-pleasing colours are: blue, green, white, purple, black, red, orange, yellow, brown and grey.

As far as stimulating interest was concerned, the range was – starting from the most stimulating and finishing with the least so – red, orange, yellow, violet, black, blue, green, white, brown and grey.

"By carefully combining colours from both sets, you can create feelings and reactions of joy, elation and excitement," he said. "And you can achieve a relaxing, comfortable, easy mood when you match a pleasing colour such as white with a low-arousal colour such as green."

Although grey comes bottom throughout, it does have its uses. "Experiments show that a person who wears a dark suit gets more respect than someone wearing a lighter colour," Professor Mehrabian said.

CONTRACEPTION

• Best and worst methods of birth control

Sterilisation remains the most effective method of birth control, according to the Alan Guttmacher Institute, an American population research corporation.

Following a massive survey, they published the following failure rates for the various methods based upon the percentage of married women who became pregnant during the first years of using them: sterilisation, 0.4 per cent; contraceptive pill, 2.4 per cent; intrauterine devices, 4.6 per cent; condom, 9.6 per cent; spermicides, 17.9 per cent; diaphragm, 18.6 per cent; rhythm method, 23.7 per cent.

The failure rates declined in later years of marriage as women become more experienced in using the methods.

COUGHING

• You can't beat hot water to soothe a COUGH

Much of the £63 million spent by Britons every year on cough medicines is just wasted money, according to experts, because the same results could have been obtained by using tried and tested home remedies such as inhaling steam or simply by going to bed early.

Commenting on a report on tests on 19 expectorants and suppressants in Which?, the Consumers' Association magazine, its editor David Dickison said: "There's no convincing evidence that expectorants work other than by providing short-term relief or a good night's sleep to help you recover." And, as far as soothing a cough, a glass of hot water had been found to be as effective as most expectorants.

• Clean your ears to cure a CHRONIC COUGH

Impacted wax in the ears can cause pressure against a nerve in the ear canal that triggers coughing which may persist for months and even years.

That's the discovery that was recently announced by Dr Fernando Martinez, assistant professor of internal medicine at the University of Michigan, who explained: "Many people are coughing needlessly because of impacted ear wax. And, they may cough as often as 25 or more times a minute. These people often mistakenly believe that the cause of their cough is an allergy, a cold, or postnasal drip – these being the most common underlying causes of chronic cough – and they often let it go on and on."

CREAM

• Cream is good for you – providing it's sour

Although cream is frowned upon by just about all nutritionists, sour cream gets the thumbs up. And, that's because it provides large amounts of both calcium and vitamin A within its 26 calories per tablespoonful.

CRYING

• Men would be healthier if they shed tears

Holding back tears might be the macho thing to do, but it could be hazardous to your health, claims a top expert.

Biochemist William Frey, of the St. Paul-Ramsey, Minnesota, Medical Center, has completed a study of 300 adults that showed that women cry five times more than men and do so on the average about once a month. "I believe that men might well be healthier if they cried more often," he said. "It appears that crying may release certain unknown chemicals that aid the body in coping with stress, and failing to cry could therefore prove to be unhealthy."

The scientist noted that whereas women usually let the 'tears fall freely', men tended to keep their tears in their eyes, not allowing them to spill out. "This desperate battle to avoid showing overt signs of emotion could well add to their stress," he explained, "making them more likely to fall victim to stress-related disorders, such as ulcers, for example."

CURRIES

• Hooked on curries? You may be addicted

You can become addicted to spicy foods because of the 'high' they can produce, reports The Medical Post in America.

There is a special substance – called capsaicin – in chilli peppers and red peppers which enhances the appreciation of food but also appears to stimulate the release of the hormone endorphin. This hormone, in turn, can create a sense of pleasure and so capsaicin can lead to an addiction to the 'highs' produced by the hormone.

CUTS

• How to make CUTS heal faster

There's a simple way to make superficial cuts, grazes and scrapes heal faster, according to a recent report in the American Journal 'Physician and Sports medicine'.

Here's what you do:

1) Clean the cut, scrape or raw skin area well.

2) Aim the output from an ordinary handheld hairdryer whose heat selector has been set to 'cool' – at the area and use it for about 10 to 15 minutes, two or three times a day, until the cut heals.

3) Be certain that the skin doesn't get too hot and keep moving the dryer about.

DANDRUFF

• The peanut oil DANDRUFF treatment

There's an old-time remedy for dandruff which has proven its efficacy in tests, according to Dr Alan Shalita, of the Dermatology

Department of State University of New York. Here's what you need to do:

First, you simply rub a small amount of slightly warm peanut oil well into your scalp. Then, after a couple of minutes or so, you apply the juice from one or more freshly squeezed lemons, leaving this on for another five minutes or so. Finally, shampoo your hair thoroughly. The treatment should be repeated once a week or so.

No one is quite certain why the peanut oil and lemon juice combination should work, except for the fact that the juice is an astringent which causes cells to shrink by precipitating proteins to their surfaces and thereby may harden and protect the scalp. "But whatever the exact mechanism may be, many of my patients have reported that this home remedy has brought them great relief," asserts Dr Shalita.

DAYDREAMS

• Daydream your troubles away

A daydream a day may well keep the doctor – as well as the psychiatrist – away.

So says Dr Henri Laborit, director of the biological research laboratory at the Boucicaut Hospital in Paris and a world renowned expert on modern-day living. "Daydreaming is not a waste of time – it's your brain telling you: 'I am overloaded, set me free for a while to recuperate.'

"And, for ten seconds or ten minutes, whatever, a daydream allows you to escape from your worries and responsibilities into a world of your own creation where everything is wonderful and fine."

Dr Laborit, who has studied the human mind for more than 30 years, first became alerted to the possible benefits of daydreaming when he observed that mentally ill patients, many of whom spend a great deal of their time in a fantasy world of their own making, seldom had cancers or infections. "This made me wonder whether their mental state helped protect them from stress, which is the root-cause of so many of today's illnesses and diseases," he explained.

His early theorising has since been confirmed by careful statistically-based research and he is now certain that we would all benefit greatly from allowing our minds to 'escape and roam free' now and then. "Obviously, you musn't carry this to an extreme," he added. "But in moderation – as all good things should be indulged in – daydreaming will do you a world of good. And, the need for this has never been as great as it is in today's world where there is but little room for imagination and creativity, and that can cause over-stressed bodies to give way to illnesses as varied as infections, cancer and heart attacks. Daydreams provide a safety valve – and in the end could even save your life."

His views are endorsed by Professor Christophe Dejours, psychiatrist and professor of work psychology at the National Conservatory of Arts and Crafts in Paris, who said: "It's vital for people's mental health that they use their imagination and the simplest way to do that is to daydream a little."

DENTISTRY

• You can save a BROKEN TOOTH

If you've broken off a tooth accidently, it can probably still be saved if you follow some important guidelines, and get professional help as quickly as possible. Here's what you should do:
• Touch the tooth as little as possible and keep the broken off bit in a moist environment. One way of doing this is to try to hold it under your tongue or snuggled against the cheek in your mouth. Alternatively, wrap the tooth in a moist tissue or towel to take it to the dentist.
• In some cases, it may be possible to replace the broken tooth on its socket and keep it there while you get help.
• In the instance of a small child – who might swallow the tooth if held in the mouth - another way of keeping it moist is to place it in a glass of milk.

The vital thing is not to let the tooth dry out as this can damage the root structure permanently, making replacement impossible. And, of course, you should hurry to the dentist's as a delay of more than an hour or so will make it all the more unlikely that the broken bit can be restored.

• Vitamin speeds healing after dental work

You will recover more quickly after dental surgery by taking extra vitamin C – which plays a vital role in healing wounds and forming bone.

Dr Winston Morris and E. Leslie Knight, Ph.D., authors of 'Balanced Nutrition Plans for Dental Patients', which has been published in America, recommend:
• If you're about to have dental work done on soft tissue, increase your vitamin C intake to 500 milligrams daily for a week before and two weeks after surgery.
• To improve bone mending, drink several glasses of skimmed milk every day in the week before and after having a tooth extracted or having root canal work done involving a bone abscess.

DEPRESSION

• Smashing remedy for DEPRESSION

A West Midlands doctor has several revolutionary remedies to help his patients reduce their stress and frustration levels as he may suggest that they:
• Smash up dinner plates.
• Stamp on flowerpots.

- Write a story.
- Go for a walk.

Explains Dr Malcolm Rigler, of Brierley Hill: "A lot of people may think I'm mad, but I've lost count of the patients who can't get off anti-depressants and tranquillisers when their real problem is simply suppressed frustration." And, taking your frustration out on innocent crockery, he added, can reduce your stress and anxiety levels, thereby perhaps warding off depression.

One patient – mother-of-two, Janice Lewry – said that the plate-breaking prescription cured her after she consulted Dr Rigler because she felt trapped at home with two young boys and "going out of my mind". "I expected to be given tranquillisers, instead he told me to buy some crockery and smash it!" she said. "And, it worked – I think Dr Rigler is brilliant."

• Phone someone to beat DEPRESSION

No, it's not an ad from British Telecom; but a top expert's advice on one way of beating the blues almost sounds as though it could be.

"When you're feeling low, call people on the telephone," says Dr Gordon Ball, director of the Behaviour Therapy Unit at New York's Cornell Medical College. "Part of depression is loneliness. Don't lose contact with others." And, he added, telephoning someone is often less stressful than visiting them.

DERMATITIS

• DERMATITIS may start in the kitchen

'Contact dermatitis' is a somewhat catch-all phrase that doctors often use to describe a rash on the hands of which the cause remains unknown.

Now it seems that the kitchen is a good place to start looking for the allergen responsible. A study recently completed by two researchers at the Skin Cancer Foundation in Sydney, Australia, looked at 14 people who had suffered hand rashes for an average of six years and found that:
- Nearly two thirds of the subjects tested positive as being allergic to contact with seafood.
- Other common allergens which provoked contact dermatitis included meats, lettuce, peppers, potatoes, pumpkins, citrus fruits, and semolina.

It's worth stressing that the allergic reactions followed mere hand contact with these foods and were not the result of eating them.

DIABETES

• Cinnamon boosts INSULIN levels

A simple spice can boost insulin levels in sufferers from diabetes, according to recent research by scientists at the US Department of Agriculture's Human Nutrition Research Center in Beltsville, Maryland.

"Cinnamon appears to contain a compound that greatly increases the effectiveness of insulin," reported biochemist Richard Anderson. "Many diabetics say that they've seen a definite improvement in their condition by using half a teaspoonful of it a day."

• Breast-feeding may prevent DIABETES

Breast-feeding is likely to prevent diabetes in babies – that's the conclusion of a recent study conducted at the Steno Memorial Hospital in Gentofte, Denmark.

The survey compared 181 children with diabetes that had been born between 1948 and 1978 with their healthy brothers and sisters totalling 94 and then comparing these groups with 6,250 children from the same age groups in the population at large.

Dr K. Borch-Johnsen, who headed the survey, reported that:
• The children with diabetes were five times more likely to have been bottle-fed than the others.
• Only two per cent of the healthy brothers and sisters of those with diabetes had never been breast-fed; this compared with 11 per cent of the diabetic children who needed insulin to control their disease.

Dr Borch-Johnsen believes that the higher rate of incidence of diabetes in the non-breast-fed children is because many, if not all, formula foods lack some of the anti-bodies and nutrients which help babies fight diabetes. "The results clearly indicate that to reduce the chances of diabetes in their children all mothers should breast-feed their babies for at least three months before switching them to a bottle," he concluded.

• 'Coated' cells may cure DIABETES

Scientists are now a step closer to curing diabetes by finding how to transplant new pancreas cells that would produce insulin naturally in the patient's body.

Dr Michael Sefton and a team at the University of Toronto in Canada have developed a technique that coats the donor's cells with plastic in such a way that the recipient's immune system will be unable to detect and reject them.

"We hope that this discovery will pave the way to the possibility of eventually curing diabetics within the next few years by transplanting coated, healthy cells," said Dr Sefton.

• Diet and exercise can get diabetics off insulin

Many diabetics would be able to get off insulin if they were to switch to a high-fibre diet and took exercise regularly, say researchers.

"Too many diabetics are on high-fat, carbohydrate restricted diets that don't provide enough fibre," explained Dr James Anderson, professor of medicine at the University of Kentucky, Lexington, USA, who has just concluded a study in which 500 diabetics went on diets that included 50 grams of fibre a day as well as being required to walk an hour a day, four days a week. "Two out of three patients were able to eliminate insulin – and their cholesterol levels fell by 30 per cent," Dr Anderson reported.

Added his co-researcher, diabetes nutritionist Cynthia Chandler: "We feel strongly that insulin is overused and that the concept that you can regulate sugar by taking more insulin is undesirable."

• How to spot the warning signs

Tens of thousands of people have diabetes and aren't aware of it. Knowing the warning signs of this disease could save your life. If you find that you have any of the following symptoms for no other obvious reason, then experts suggest that you should consult your doctor:

• Excessive urination, either as a marked increase in frequency or amount.

• Increased fluid intake, such as suddenly starting to drink considerably more liquids.

• Excessive hunger reflected by a marked increase in the need for food throughout the day.

• Unexplained tiredness. This may manifest itself as a constant sense of fatigue or sleeping 10 or more hours at night and still feeling tired afterwards.

• Substantial weight fluctuation. This can be either weight gain or loss.

Other signs that could indicate diabetes include: increased craving for sweet drinks, blurred vision, tingling or numbness in the feet or hands, dry or flaky skin, vaginal itching, frequent skin infections, slow healing of cuts or bruises, nausea, and irritability.

Hypoglycaemia – which describes the state which results when a diabetic has an insufficient intake of carbohydrate may also cause the following symptoms: severe hunger, nervousness, anxiety, shakiness, and rapid or irregular heartbeats.

Testing for possible diabetes can be done through simple urine or blood tests and anyone who has reason to believe that he or she might be affected should see their doctor.

• When GERMAN MEASLES can also mean DIABETES

The chances of contracting diabetes later in life are greater if you've been exposed to German measles before birth, says Dr John Sever, of the National Institute of Allergy and Infectious Diseases in Bethesda, Maryland, USA.

"There is a definite link between

the two," he said, "and the virus can lead to diabetes in 20 to 40 per cent of those affected. While other problems in the unborn resulting from German measles – such as possible deafness, heart disease, cataracts or central nervous system abnormalities – usually show up soon after birth, the diabetes may not appear for 20 or more years afterwards.

"If you know that you've been exposed to German measles, then it's a very good idea to be particularly aware of any symptoms which might indicate diabetes so that the disease can be caught and treated at an early stage," he added.

DIAGNOSIS

• Tell-tale toilet

Japanese scientists are developing a 'toilet sensor' which analyses urine to assess various aspects of the user's state of health. "We expect that the 'smart loo' will be able to provide a daily health check as well as early diagnosis of disease," say the researchers. "And, it will even be able to print out its findings when connected to a home computer."

DIARRHOEA

• Fruit concentrate can banish DIARRHOEA

Simple fruit concentrate added to contaminated water can kill the E. coli bacteria that causes diarrhoea, says Dr Michael Gracey, head of a research team in Perth, Australia.

"And, there's even some evidence that the concentrate can also kill the bacteria responsible for cholera, one of the world's most devastating diseases," he added.

He said that travellers in parts of the world where the purity of the water is suspect could protect themselves by adding the fruit concentrate to a container of water, allowing the mixture to stand at room temperature for an hour, and then refrigerating it.

DIETING

• Dieting isn't DEPRESSING!

Many people keep on postponing going on a diet because they fear that this will make them feel low and depressed – but cutting down on food can actually lift your spirits instead, says an expert.

"Completely contrary to the widespread myth that dieting causes depression, it can actually boost your mood," said American psychiatrist Jack Leedy. Proof of this effect is to be found in the results of a recent study at the University of Pittsburgh involving 76 subjects who took part in a dieting programme. The participants lost an average of 12 pounds over 10 weeks and they became clearly less depressed and experienced noticeable improvements in mood as they shed weight.

Explained Dr Leedy: "These people became less depressed

because as you lose weight, you get to think more of yourself – your self-esteem goes up – and that fights depression.

"Most people who are overweight are depressed about it, and the longer they avoid dieting and putting on weight, the more depressed they become. But as soon as they start losing weight – in fact, as soon as they actually decide to go on a diet they banish that depression."

Dr Leedy did warn, however, that some diets could indeed create depression. "Some of the more kooky diets, which have people concentrating on one food, skip certain meals, or fast altogether, can certainly make you depressed," he said. "But a sensible, balanced diet will have exactly the opposite effect, it will be a real mood booster."

• Fried vegetables absorb more fat than meat

If you're on a diet, you'd be well advised to pass up on any meal involving fried vegetables because these have been shown to absorb more of the fat that they're cooked in than meat, according to a study at the University of California.

The worst offender in soaking up fat is the eggplant which can absorb 83 grams of fat in only 70 seconds of frying, more than four times as much as an equal portion of potatoes.

Meat, on the other hand, absorbs relatively little fat when fried,

mainly because it is higher in fat to start with.

• Seven easy ways to make you stick to your diet

Even the best motivated of us are at times tempted to break the rules when we're on a slimming diet - but the following seven strategies developed by a top weight control expert can help keep you on the straight and narrow.

"These strategies have been tested on many hundreds of patients and have been found to be most effective at preventing them from 'pigging out' when their diets are getting on top of them," says Professor Maria Simonson, director of the health, weight and stress reduction programme at John Hopkins School of Medicine in America. These are her recommendations:

1) Consume as few calories as you can in a liquid form as solid foods provide greater satisfaction.

2) Drink a large glass of water about half an hour before your meals. This calorie-free 'first course' will make you feel less hungry when you sit down to eat.

3) Eat a salad – with a low-calorie dressing – some ten minutes before the meal as this will also curb your appetite.

4) Never allow yourself to get really ravenously hungry before a meal as this is likely to cause you to overeat. If absolutely necessary, it's better to have a small snack to keep the

hunger pangs at bay.

5) Schedule your meals for fixed times each and every day – and stick to that routine! You'll find that your body will soon adjust to its new timetable and you'll have fewer cravings for food between the set mealtimes.

6) Try using a cocktail fork. The smaller fork will force you to eat more slowly. The slower you eat, the less food it takes for you to feel filled up.

7) Don't be a martyr and give up all your favourite foods as the frustration of doing this may build up to such an extent that you blow your whole diet. Allow yourself the occasional treat, but ration yourself to small servings.

• Start dieting the easy way

Sticking to a weight-reducing diet will be easier for women if they start it during the first two weeks of their menstrual cycle. "The level of the hormone oestrogen – which also acts as an appetite suppressant – is higher during that time," explained Dr Phillippa Wall, of the University of Sydney, Australia. "And, that means that it will be less stressful for dieters to cope with a reduced intake of food in the first instance, thereby increasing their chances of maintaining their diet."

• The first diet book

The current obsession with slimming is hardly a new fad because the first successful diet book was written nearly 130 years

ago by William Banting, Queen Victoria's official court undertaker, when he noted that fat people tended to die younger than thin ones.

His book – 'A Letter on Corpulence Addressed to the Public' – was a great success and went through three editions. And, for a while, the word 'banting' was used as a synonym for dieting in honour of the author. A man who took his own advice, Banting who weighed nearly 15 stone when he wrote the book at the age of 60, slimmed down to just over 10 stone and lived to be 81.

• Two tips to lose EXTRA WEIGHT

Whether you eat breakfast or not as well as the time you choose to exercise can strongly influence the efficiency of your weight-reduction programme, according to experts.

Dieters who skip breakfast could end up gaining weight instead of losing it, warned Dr Wayne Calloway, of George Washington University, who explained that people who don't eat breakfast usually have a metabolic rate four to five per cent lower than normal. "Because of this lower rate, their bodies don't burn fat as efficiently," he said. "And, as a result of this metabolic slump, a dieter who starts skipping breakfast could expect to gain as much as one pound, even if otherwise his or her daily calorie intake remains constant."

As far as losing weight by burning

off calories is concerned, this will be more efficient if you work out before a meal instead of after one. A study at Mount Sinai Hospital in New York showed that overweight subjects burned significantly more calories when they exercised on an empty stomach than when they exercised after a meal. Strangely enough, the situation was exactly the reverse for people who were already lean; they burned more by exercising shortly after eating.

• How low is low-fat?

Don't believe all the claims that you read on food packaging because more often than not they're just marketing ploys.

That's the conclusion of a recent report by Which? magazine that found that there often is no evidence to support claims that the foods are truly 'low-salt', 'low-fat', or 'high-fibre'.

"These claims have no legal definition – manufacturers can use them as they like," said the magazine, adding that when these statements were used responsibly, they can help you eat more healthily. "Used irresponsibly, they're a con," the report added.

• The wonders of porridge

A team of researchers has confirmed what mothers in Scotland have been saying for generations – porridge is really terribly good for you.

According to Dr James Anderson at Kentucky University, the main reason why porridge can help make you healthier in a wide variety of ways is because it's such a rich source of soluble fibre. This means that porridge is good for dieters because it aids in keeping the lower intestinal tract clear. Additionally, it can help by reducing cholesterol levels as well as lowering blood pressure.

"And, an often overlooked benefit of porridge, is that it really can assist people on a diet eat less because although being low in calories it is so filling that it stops them nibbling snacks between meals," he added.

DOCTORS

• Ten questions you should ask your doctor

You can get better medical care if you know how to get the most out of your doctor – that's the advice of Dr Cynthia Carver, a Toronto, Canada, government medical officer and author of 'Patient Beware!' which has recently been published in America. And, as her comments are just as relevant to patients in Britain, here are her top tips:

• When choosing a doctor, look for one that doesn't rush you in and out of the office.

• Ensure that your doctor takes the time to find out about your lifestyle, eating and drinking habits, as well as special worries or stresses you may have at work or at home.

And, when you see your doctor about a specific problem, these are the 10 questions that you should ask if they're not already answered during the earlier part of the consultation:

l) What do I have? (Finding out the correct medical name of your problem will make it easier for you to find more details about it in books.)
2) What is the cause of it?
3) What is the usual course of this illness, disease or problem?
4) Is this likely to affect other parts of my body?
5) Could I have something else – that is, another problem which could cause similar symptoms to appear?
6) What's the best treatment in my case?
7) For how long and how often will I have to take the treatment, medication, etc? And, how long will it take before it's likely to show results?
8) Are there any possible side-effects of which I should be aware? Can this treatment possibly interact unfavourably with any medication I'm taking currently?
9) Are there any other ways of treating the problem? And, are these more, or less safe, than the one you suggest?
10) What would happen if I didn't treat the problem?

"Learn as much as possible about your disease or problem," Dr Carver added. "Doctors can make mistakes and your best defence against this possibility is knowledge. The key to receiving careful medical treatment lies in being a well-informed consumer."

• The risks of being a GP

Family doctors are facing an ever-increasing risk of violence, according to a recent survey which found that one in twelve doctors had been the victims of attacks within the past two years. Apart from those actually suffering violence at the hands of patients or their relatives, nearly half of the doctors had been threatened, often in their own surgeries.

The survey – conducted by Electoral Reform Ballot Services – was based on the answers provided by 2,000 doctors in London, but it is thought that similar results would have been obtained in other parts of the country. Commented Dr Ian Bogle on behalf of the British Medical Association: "These figures are the first real measures of the problem and I am absolutely horrified."

DRIVING

• When green says stop

An adhesive skin patch measuring less than an inch across is the latest weapon in combating drunken driving.

The smart patch is white to start with but turns to a bright green when stuck to the skin of someone whose blood alcohol level is above the limit for driving. "It can either be used to test other people, or a driver might choose to test themself so as to know when they shouldn't get behind the wheel of a car," said a spokesman for Dermal Systems International, the American company which owns the patent.

The tell-tale patch is currently being tested in the States and is expected to go on sale there later this year after which the manufacturers hope to introduce it in Britain.

• Keeping awake to stay alive

Nodding off at the wheel while driving on today's busy roads is an almost certain way to end up becoming a traffic statistic. Here are some tips to help keep you awake when you travel:

• Drink plenty of coffee or caffeinated soft drinks. If you're hungry, have a small snack, not a full course meal which would only make you sleepy.

• Listen to an interesting talk show or upbeat music on the radio. Avoid soft, soothing instrumental music which can make you drowsy.

• Reduce smoking – it produces carbon monoxide which slows down your reaction time.

• Don't sit too long in one position. Stop the car every hour or two and stretch your legs with a short walk.

• If possible, avoid all medication. Even over-the-counter cold remedies can impair your driving.

• Open the windows – a breath of fresh air will help keep you alert.

DRUG ABUSE

• The perils of trying to look sexy

Many of today's youngsters are using potentially lethal anabolic steroids in an effort to look 'sexier', warns Dr Douglas Williamson, a psychiatrist at the Crichton Royal Hospital in Dumfries.

But, apart from the very real health risks they're taking, the results are often hardly what the users expected, he said, because the drugs often lowered the men's sex drive and gave girls a deep voice and hairy chest. Dr Williamson's survey found that four per cent of the men and one per cent of the women interviewed admitted having used body-building steroids for cosmetic reasons. One man even said that he'd resorted to the drugs just to "look better in his wedding photos".

"But in reality these drugs won't help you succeed with the opposite sex," Dr Williamson added. "Quite the reverse, they will damage you sexually and can also lead to liver failure and premature heart attacks."

DRUNKENNESS

• Beware the drinking pedestrian

Although everyone is aware

nowadays of the dangers of drinking and driving, there's another almost as lethal a menace on the roads, and that's the drunken pedestrian.

The menace of the 'drink-walker' is highlighted in a recent report from the Transport and Road Research Laboratory which estimated that 560 pedestrians killed in one year had been drinking before their accident and that nearly three quarters of them had blood/alcohol levels above the legal limit for drivers.

Another alarming statistic was that many of these pedestrians were not actually crossing the road at the time and that the highest alcohol concentrations were found in those who were killed while walking in the carriageway with their backs to the traffic.

So there could be a strong case for saying: "No more for me, I'm walking tonight."

to view right into the middle ear and so identify infections and tumours as well as look for leakages from the inner ear which are a frequent cause of dizziness.

To introduce the endoscope into the middle ear, a small slit has to be made in the eardrum, but this heals quickly afterwards.

"Doctors have been using endoscopes in the ear for many years, but this was just to look at the outer parts, such as the eardrum or the ear canal," explained Dr Dennis Poe, who designed the new technique. "Looking further into the ear wasn't practical until it was possible to make endoscopes smaller. Now I've been able to stop doing exploratory surgery on patients to look for causes of middle ear disorders."

Another advantage of the new procedure is that it is much less invasive and this reduces the chances of infection.

EAR INFECTIONS

- **New procedure can avoid EAR SURGERY**

A newly-developed technique may save thousands of patients from having to undergo surgery to diagnose middle ear disorder.

Using a miniature telescope – called an 'endoscope' – the procedure developed at the world-famous Lahey Clinic in Burlington, Mass., USA, makes it possible for a doctor

ENERGY

- **How to face each new day with energy to burn**

Do you envy those people who bounce gleefully out of bed in the morning, just raring to go and filled with zestful energy to deal with whatever the day will bring? Well, you can join their ranks by following some advice from two top experts – Dr Jack Leedy, staff psychiatrist at Lutheran Medical

Center, and nutritionist Dr H. L. Newbolt, both of New York – who jointly have compiled a list of dos and don'ts to be heeded by those who would like to feel more with it in the morning.

• DO have a good wholesome dinner in the evening.

• DON'T eat or have a snack shortly before you go to bed as this will spur the digestive system into action and could keep you awake or just make your sleep less restful.

• DO get the right amount of sleep, this usually being between six and eight hours for most healthy adults.

• DON'T sleep too little or too much – either will make you feel tired when you get up. Find out by experimentation what your optimum amount of sleep is and stick to it.

• DO delay going to bed until you're tired enough to be ready to nod off once you hit the sheets.

• DON'T lie around in bed once you wake up fully.

• DO some brief physical exercises when you get up to stimulate your body into action, following this up with a refreshing shower to wash away any remaining weariness.

• DON'T skip breakfast as your body needs the nutrient intake to keep you feeling fit throughout the morning. So have a glass of fruit juice – which is an excellent energiser – and some high-fibre cereal as well as a piece of fruit.

• DO take brief five-minute breaks at work to stop your fatigue level from building up. If possible, when taking a break change your environment even by as little as taking a short walk down the hall and try not to think about work problems.

EXERCISE

• Getting fit is miracle cure

A good work-out is one doctor's cure for all sorts of ailments. Dr David Hanraty, of Hailsham, East Sussex, writes out fitness prescriptions for his patients, telling them to go to the local fitness centre three times a week for ten weeks. "And, the prescriptions specify the exercise regimen we want the patient to follow," he says. "It could be swimming, yoga or gym workouts. And, the results have been remarkable since we started doing this 18 months ago. Not only do patients get fitter, they also get better from their illnesses." Included among the doctor's successes are:

• A former drinker and smoker who now cycles and runs as well as saving £4,000 a year on alcohol and cigarettes.

• A 76-year-old asthmatic woman who was unable to walk any distance before becoming breathless and who can now enjoy a two-mile stroll.

• A diabetic woman who was also clinically depressed who lost two stone and found herself a job after years of unemployment.

The scheme is so successful that health authorities from various other parts of the country have shown interest in copying it.

• The old fashioned way to keep fit

Exercise experts are pitching an old fashioned sport for staying in shape – horseshoes.

Seen through the eyes of today's jogging and aerobics fanatics, the backyard game may seem too lazy and gentle, but doctors say that the bending, walking and stretching it involves is very good for you. And, it's also much safer than most other sports or exercises.

"Playing horseshoes is a great way to keep fit because it enhances one's physical sense of well-being, is of minimal risk, and can even be played safely by the elderly," said Dr Basil Clyman, of the Veterans Hospital in Sepulveda, California. "What's more, the sport requires a great deal of coordination and concentration while remaining a good way to relax mentally."

• The truth about exercise

How knowledgeable are you about exercise? Take this quick true-or-false quiz devised by Alabama's Auburn University experts to find out.

1) You should never consume liquids when engaged in strenuous exercise.

2) Any exercise programme which is likely to do any good is going to take up a lot of your time.

3) If you run a mile you'll burn up more calorie.s than if you walk the same distance.

4) If you exercise regularly, you'll not only feel better physically, but you'll also get some psychological benefits.

Answers: 1) False because drinking will cut down the extent of the dehydration caused by prolonged heavy sweating and this will reduce the risk of heat stroke; 2) False because there is no need to engage in lengthy exercise sessions to gain benefits. For most people, 20 to 40 minutes of exercising three times a week is enough; 3) False as you'll use just about the same number of calories covering a mile whether you walk, run, or jog; 4) True because surveys have shown that people who exercise regularly also usually enjoy greater self-esteem, less anxiety, and may even get relief from mild occasional depression.

• Twice a week is enough

How much exercise do you really need to keep you fit providing you're so in the first place? Amazingly enough, recent research has shown that you only need to exercise twice a week to maintain your peak fitness and that you won't do any better by working at it more frequently.

That's the surprise result of a study conducted by American cardiologists Dr Charles Kanakis and Dr Robert Hickson, according to a report in the 'Journal of Cardiac Rehabilitation'.

The study was based on 12 healthy adult volunteers who were first put through an intensive 10-week long training programme to whip them into top physical condition. Exercising for 40 minutes a day, six days a week, the volunteers jogged and used exercise machines to reach their fitness peak which was measured by recordings of their lung capacity and resting pulse rate.

The volunteers were then split into two groups of six each. For the next 15 weeks, one group exercised for only two 40-minute sessions a week. The other group did the same exercises, but for four sessions a week, or twice as much.

When the subjects were tested again at the end of the study, the researchers found that all 12 had maintained the same level of physical fitness.

"This surprisingly proves that you need to exercise only twice weekly to stay in shape physically," commented Dr Kanakis. "Once you attain your fitness goal, a twice a week maintenance programme is just as effective as a four-time-a-week regimen."

• Why you shouldn't stop EXERCISE suddenly

You should never stop any strenuous physical exercise or activity suddenly and remain in a standing position, warns Dr Stephen Langer, president of the American Nutritional Medical Association.

"If you remain upright while your body tries to adapt to the changing demands made upon it, you could increase your risk of developing heartbeat irregularities and suffering from a decreased oxygen supply to the heart," he explained.

• You'll run faster if someone watches you

Joggers who would like to increase their running speed should simply run where they're watched by other people.

That's the conclusion of psychologist Charles Worringham, of the University of Wisconsin in Madison, USA, who filmed 36 male and female joggers and found that they all ran faster when they thought someone was watching them. "The increase in pace probably occurs because the joggers want to make themselves look better to the spectators," he said.

• You'll workout better at home

Forget attending aerobic classes and workout at home instead because then you'll be more likely to stick to your exercise programme and attain your fitness goals – that's the message from Stanford University following a study of 357 'couch potatoes' who decided to improve their fitness.

One group went to exercise classes two or three times a week while another did their exercises at home, aided by the moral support of a phone call once a month from researchers checking on how they were doing. Both groups achieved roughly the same physical results while they stuck with the exercises, but those who trained at home stayed with their programmes longer, eventually attaining higher goals.

EYE DROPS

• Take EYE DROPS this way to stave off side-effects

Many eye drops can cause serious side-effects – but you can avoid these by putting in the drops correctly.

The side-effects can occur because most drops are designed for topical use – that is local application – but if you use them carelessly they may become absorbed systematically, that is within the body generally. "And, the side-effects of some drops can be potentially very severe," warned Dr Zimmerman, chairman of ophthalmology at the University of Louisville School of Medicine. "They can include cardiac arrhythmias, angina, asthma, increased blood pressure, to name but a few."

You can however avoid these dangers by using the drops correctly as follows:

• Place a finger in the inner corner of one eye and exert gentle pressure into the corner.
• Put the drops in the eye while continuing to apply pressure with your finger and hold this for two to three minutes.
• Repeat the procedure for the other eye. The use of this simple technique will stop the drops from entering into the tear ducts and thereby keep their effects restricted to the area for which they're intended.

EYESIGHT

• Seeing spots?

This is what you need to know! Are you seeing spots floating around in your field of vision now and then? Well, it's nothing to worry about and something that will happen to just about all of us sooner or later, says a top expert.

Typically, the spots – known as 'floaters' – will be distinguished most clearly when you're looking towards bright light, a light background, or even at a blue sky. And, as you try to look at the spots themselves, they will appear to move, either slowly drifting or quickly darting away as you move your eyes.

"The spots are the result of some of the vitreous humour – that's the jelly-like substance that fills the eyes – beginning to liquidify, something that occurs as we become older," explains Dr Alfonse Cinotti, chairman of the department of ophthalmology at New Jersey Medical School. "As this takes place, it's quite common for small pieces of the gel to become separated from the eye's inner surface and end up floating around in the eye itself. When light enters the eye, these small particles of gel cast minute shadows on the retina, the light-sensitive membrane at the back of the eye.

"What you're seeing is not the particles themselves, but rather the shadows they cast," Dr Cinotti said, adding "that floaters were harmless, but that there were other visual symptoms that you should have checked out if you experience them."

For example, if you were to see flashes of light inside the eye, this could indicate a torn retina, something that requires urgent medical attention. Some types of flashing light, often zigzag-shaped, are, of course, symptoms of an oncoming migraine-type headache.

Although observing occasional floaters now and then is not usually a problem, you should always seek expert opinion if you have a dramatic increase in the number of spots you see or experience any kind of unusual sight problem, such as sudden blurring or loss or vision of any kind.

Oddity note: A 17th Century Italian nobleman became so intrigued by the intricate variety of the floaters in his eyes that he had a special chamber constructed with a brightly lit light blue background so that he could observe them more clearly. As he became older, he spent most of his time in the chamber looking at the spots that danced in his eyes.

• Beware of the bright sun

Maybe there's something to be said for Britain's often overcast sky after all because research has revealed that Florida's bright sunshine may be contributing to the failing eyesight of many of its elderly residents.

Ordinary light from the sun could be causing the loss of retinal cells usually associated with ageing, explained Dr Theodore Williams, professor of biological science at Florida State University at Tallahassee.

"We've long known that extremely bright light can kill cells in the eye, but now it appears that simply being exposed to light of ordinary intensity can also be harmful," he said.

• One in eight drivers fail eye test

Twelve per cent of motorists do not meet the basic standard of sight laid down in the Highway Code which requires them to read a normal number plate with either eye at 25 yards. The shock finding was made during a survey of more than 3,000 drivers conducted by opticians Dollond & Aitchison. The over-sixties did worst in the survey with nearly half of them failing to meet the standard and the second worst result recorded was that of drivers aged 50 to 60 years of which just under a third didn't pass the number plate test. Fifty per cent of those tested had never had an eye test before.

• The potato cure for sore eyes

Here's a simple home remedy for eyes that are sore and swollen from lack of sleep or because of an allergy. Cut a raw potato into quarter inch thick slices and put a slice over each closed eyelid while you relax for about ten minutes. The potatoes have the natural ability to absorb excess water and thereby reduce puffiness.

FATIGUE

• Two ways to beat FATIGUE

Feeling tired and run down? Instead of reaching for yet another cup of coffee, try a traditional natural pick-me-up by eating a handful of raw, unsalted sunflower seeds.

Another time-honoured way to beat tiredness – and one which is used by many athletes – is to have some bee pollen. If you decide to try this last one, you should start with a very small dose indeed – just a couple of granules or so for the first couple of days – because some people are allergic to pollen. If the low dosage doesn't produce any allergic reaction, you can gradually increase your intake to up to half a teaspoonful.

Both raw sunflower seeds and bee pollen are available at most health food shops.

FERTILITY

• Ill-conceived baby planning

A recent survey by the Family Planning Association has revealed 'widespread ignorance' on the part of many couples about conception.

FPA director Doreen Massey said: "Women are not being given basic information about when they are fertile, how often they should have sex if they want to get pregnant, or even about the mechanics of conception." For example, she said, many women believe that they will not get pregnant if their periods are not in a strict 28-day cycle, little realising that a normal cycle can vary as much as from 21 to 42 days.

There was also a great deal of misinformation about how to conceive with "many couples expecting a pregnancy as soon as they stop using contraception," she added. "Many fear they are infertile when there is nothing wrong. It is up to the doctors to provide more information and reassurance."

FIBRE

• When fibre can be harmful

Eating too much of the wrong fibre can actually contribute to bone damage. That's the conclusion of nutritionist Dr Alison Avenell, of the Aberdeen-based Rowett Research Institute, who warned that taking in large quantities of high-fibre cereals could interfere with the body's ability to take in calcium and thereby lead to a serious loss of minerals in the bones.

Dr Avenell added that post-menopausal women might be particularly at risk from this effect as would be women who went on frequent diets and then ate high-fibre cereals to ease hunger pangs. Her advice: "It's generally better to get your fibre from fruit and vegetables than from too many cereals which are rich in bran."

FISHING

• How not to get hooked

Every year hundreds of people injure themselves – some times badly – while handling fish-hooks. Here's how to avoid the problem: store the hooks between two strips of masking or transparent sticky tape to keep them safely in place and avoid wounds.

FOOD CRAVINGS

• The 5-D plan to beat food cravings

If you're on a diet and get sudden food cravings, here's a simple five-point plan devised by Working Mother magazine in the United States that will stop you from giving in too easily:

1) DELAY reaching for what you crave for at least 10 minutes to ensure that your decision is a conscious one and not just the result of a temporary impulse.

2) DISTRACT yourself by deliberately starting a new task that requires concentration and may take your mind off the craving.

3) DISTANCE yourself from the food you're craving. If at home, leave the kitchen; in a restaurant, ask the waiter to remove it.

4) DETERMINE whether you really and truly want to give in to your craving; and if the answer is and remains yes . . .

5) DECIDE firmly just how large a portion you're going to allow yourself to have. Then have it, enjoy it fully, but don't allow yourself to go back for more.

FOOT ODOUR

• Home remedies for FOOT ODOUR

If you've got an occasional problem with foot odour - which usually results from perspiration reacting with bacteria on the skin - these tips may help:

• Choose socks that are made from natural fibres as they are more absorbent than synthetic ones.

• Don't just wash the socks, but boil them to kill any bacteria.

- Try wearing two pairs of socks with cotton next to the skin. Cooling and ventilation will be promoted by the air spaces between the socks.
- When you wash your feet, be sure to dry very carefully and thoroughly between the toes.
- Be careful what you eat. Some foods – curries, garlic, chilli, peppers and onions – can exude oils that can be excreted in the sweat glands of your feet.
- Crushed sage sprinkled in your shoes is good at absorbing odours if replaced every few days.

FOOTWEAR

- **High-tech running shoes can ruin your feet**

Those very expensive high-tech, state-of-the-art running shoes can actually be bad for your feet, according to a study completed at Montreal's Concordia University.

"Some of the worst examples are actual safety hazards rather than protective devices," concluded the researchers who found that athletes wearing the high-tech footwear were more likely to suffer more injuries to their feet than those wearing ordinary sneakers. The reason for this? Apparently the expensive shoes have so much cushioning built in that wearers who injure their feet, don't even know it, and play on making their condition worse.

FRUIT

- **An apple a day can keep the surgeon away . . . And, so can oatmeal and dill pickles!**

Eating a piece of fruit every day can reduce your risk of contracting stomach cancer by up to a half, says Dr David Forman, of the Imperial Cancer Fund, who believes that diet could be as important a cause of the disease as smoking.

"If everyone were to eat 30 per cent more apples, oranges or bananas, Britain's annual death toll from this type of cancer could be cut to about 6,500 from the present 9,800," he said, adding "that experts are still trying to work out which parts of our diets increase the risks. Some of the answers to that question should be forthcoming in 10 years when a massive study involving more than 250,000 volunteers in seven European countries will be completed."

More evidence of how what you eat can affect your health risks came from American experts who discovered that – along with apples and other fruit – oatmeal and dill pickles can also help keep the surgeon away.

Oatmeal can assist in keeping your blood pressure at a safe level, according to Dr James Anderson, head of a research team at the University of Kentucky, who added: "No one knows what kind of fibre is most effective in lowering blood pressure, but water-soluble fibres – found in oats, beans and other vegetables – lower cholesterol and insulin levels. And, when insulin levels fall, it is easier for the body to get rid of salt. A bowl of oatmeal and three bran muffins a day can lower your pressure by ten per cent."

Eating dill pickles can also reduce your cholesterol, said Dr Joseph Wegyvary, a Texas scientist, who explained: "These pickles contain large quantities of pectin and aluminium – both ingredients help acids in bile to absorb cholesterol and aid in efficiently eliminating it with body wastes."

GARLIC

• The pros and cons of garlic

Garlic is one of the world's oldest medicines and, according to many alternative health practitioners, one of the best. However, there is another side to the coin, and it seems that garlic can also cause all sorts of undesirable and even dangerous side-effects. Here are some of the facts about garlic:

HOW IT MAY HELP YOU

Garlic's antibiotic properties, which have been confirmed since the 1920s by numerous animal and human studies, has been found to be helpful by many to:

• Reduce high blood pressure.

• Cure minor instances of food poisoning or indigestion.
• Alleviate bladder and urinary infections.
• Relieve pain in arthritic patients.
• Reduce cholesterol levels as well as minimising the chances of blood clots developing.
• Additionally, garlic juice applied externally has been credited with clearing minor skin infections.

While most of these beneficial effects haven't been fully proven scientifically, there is sufficient anecdotal evidence to substantiate garlic's claim to be the leading natural remedy for a variety of ailments. But . . .

HOW IT MAY HARM YOU

"Garlic can cause a wide array of gastrointestinal problems, including heartburn, belching, flatulence and stomach ulcers," says Dr Varro Tyler, a natural drug specialist and professor at Purdue University in America. "Eating too much garlic - and too much in this context means six or eight cloves daily - will make you ill. And, those who are extra sensitive might have problems with an even smaller intake with some individuals developing allergic reactions, such as hives, and even asthma."

Another warning comes from Dr William Epstein, professor of dermatology at the University of California at San Francisco, who said: "Coming into contact with garlic can cause an outbreak of dermatitis as it contains substances that can trigger off the disease."

When expert opinion is so conflicting, it's difficult to draw a hard and fast conclusion about garlic, but the best advice is that if you choose to take it as a supplement rather than as an occasional spice in food – you should do so very carefully and ideally after having consulted your doctor first.

GASTROENTERITIS

• The end to tummy aches?

British scientists say that they're close to finding the answer to violent tummy upsets.

The hope for a cure for gastroenteritis follows the discovery of a genetic blueprint for the bug that causes it. This means that it will now he possible for experts to test for the virus which brings about the typical severe vomiting, diarrhoea and flu-like symptoms associated with it.

More importantly, it also means that it's now much more likely that a vaccine may be developed to counter gastroenteritis.

"And, this could also prevent the infectious virus from spreading in hospitals, cruise ships and schools," reported Dr Ian Clarke, from the microbiology department at the University of Southampton, where the discovery was made.

"The viruses, as well as being passed from person to person, are also transmitted through environmental contamination of food and water," he explained. "Water-borne outbreaks have been reported from contaminated municipal water, private water supplies, and in swimming pools. Virus contamination of sea water has also been suspected. We'll be able to develop clinical tests where you could test one oyster from a bed and see if it was contaminated, or the water from a beach to warn swimmers."

Apart from signalling the beginning of the end for tummy ache, the discovery may also bring millions of pounds to the university if it can market test kits to give a clean bill of health to hotels, resorts and other similar businesses.

GUM DISEASE

• Are you at risk from GUM DISEASE?

Researchers in America have isolated several factors which make people more likely to suffer from gum disease. If you're affected by any of the following, then it's strongly recommended that you should see your dentist regularly for your twice-yearly checkups, according to the publication 'Dental Health Adviser'.

Drugs or medications. Some medicines reduce the flow of saliva as a side-effect and if you're taking any of these, your chance of gum disease are greater because normal saliva has an anti-bacterial action and gum-attacking bacteria spread more rapidly in a dry mouth. Additionally, any drugs that reduce your immune system's ability to reject infection also increase the possibility of gum disease.

Hormones. Women who are pregnant or who are taking birth control pills were also found to have a higher incidence of gum problems.

Smoking. People who smoke – whether cigarettes, cigars or a pipe – are more prone to gum disease than those who don't. Part of the reason for this is that tobacco can create a sticky film on the teeth on which bacteria can cling and grow. Incidentally, the risk is also higher for those who chew tobacco.

Diet. What you choose to eat also greatly affects your gums. The greater your intake of sugary, starchy foods, the greater your chance of having trouble in the mouth.

Emotional factors. Various emotions – including stress, anxiety and depression – may make your mouth dry up and promote gum disease.

Other diseases. The chances of gum inflammation are greater for those people who suffer from diabetes as well as those who have certain thyroid and other endocrine gland disorders.

Irritation in the month. Gums can become irritated by a number of physical causes, including food that gets trapped by bad fillings, dentures that fit poorly, or just not enough correct brushing.

The inheritance factor. Genetics seem to play a big role in determining how likely you're to have gum problems. You're almost certainly more susceptible if your parents had the disorder.

HEADACHES

- **Five common HEADACHE myths exposed**

If there is one subject upon which each individual sufferer feels that he or she is an expert, that surely must be headaches.

This idea of 'every man his own expert' has however led to many widespread myths about the problem, according to Dr Lee Kudrow, who has done special research on headaches at the University of California in Los Angeles. "And, some of this false information can actually be harmful because it stops the patient from getting the right advice." Here are some of the most common myths:

- Migraine sufferers have a specific type of personality that brings on the pain.
- Smog is the cause of chronic headaches.
- The reason why women have more headaches than men is because they're emotionally unstable.
- If you've got a pain in the head, you should always take drugs to relieve it.

• Children often develop headaches because they want to attract attention.

"Each and every one of these statements is totally untrue," declared Dr Kudrow. "So don't base what you do about your headache or migraine upon any of these myths. Instead, if your pains are frequent or severe, seek medical help."

• Hairbrush your headache away

You can brush away your tension headache, says Dr Seymour Diamond, director of the Diamond Headache Clinic in Chicago. Here's how you go about it: Choose a hairbrush that's not too hard nor too soft and begin at the temples just above the eyebrow line. Gently move the brush in small circles against the scalp and gradually work your way to the back of the head and the upper part of the neck. Repeat on the other side, then move on to the top of the head until you've brushed all of it. Remember to always use the brush slowly and gently without too much force.

• Painkillers can make HEADACHES worse

Taking too many painkillers to control your headaches may in fact make them worse as well as increase their frequency, warns Dr Alan Rapoport, director of the New England Center for Headache in Greenwich, Connecticut, USA.

"Patients who regularly took five or more pain relief pills or tablets for their headaches found that both the severity and the number of headaches reduced after they cut their intake of medication," he said, adding: "It's a vicious circle. You have frequent headaches, so you take a lot of medication – but this may actually make things worse for you in the long-term."

• Swinging way to cure a headache

There's an ancient Chinese technique called 'Li Shou' which can help you get rid of tension headaches – or at least considerably reduce their intensity – by simply swinging your arms, say two American experts.

"There's no need to take drugs for most tension headaches," says Dr Edward Chang, chairman of the department of psychology and special education at Albany State College in Georgia. "The hand-swinging treatment really works and, despite its ancient origins, is based on scientifically valid principles because it redirects blood flow away from your head, relieving the pressure on artery walls that have contracted with tension. The result – no more headache."

And, the 'cure' is heartily endorsed by Dr James Giannini, professor of psychiatry at Northeastern Ohio Universities College of Medicine, who explained: "It's a simple exercise that both diverts blood flow from the brain and releases endorphins – the body's own natural morphine – resulting in stress reduction and headache relief."

These are Dr Chang's step-by-step instructions for performing Li Shou:
• Stand up and relax. Place your feet about two feet apart with the toes pointing forward. Let your hands hang naturally at your sides. Close your eyes but focus them mentally towards your feet.
• Remain as relaxed as possible as you extend both arms backwards until they're at waist level behind you. Using an easy pendulum-like rhythm, keep swinging your arms back and forth. Don't force the degree of swing to increase it beyond what is comfortable.
• Keep up the exercise for at least 100 swings while retaining a steady rate of swinging. In the unlikely event that the swinging makes you feel dizzy or makes the headache worse, stop.

• Tonight please, I've got a HEADACHE

Making love can help cure a headache. A new study in America has found that more than a third of women experienced significant relief from headaches after making love, with 26 per cent reporting long-lasting relief and a further 10 per cent saying that they had experienced at least temporary relief.

In another study, sexual activity brought 'moderate to complete relief' to one quarter of migraine sufferers and some relief to another quarter, according to Dr James Couch, professor of neurology at Southern Illinois University School of Medicine.

Experts analysing the data are theorising that the relief occurs because the brain releases pain-killing chemicals during sexual intercourse.

HEALTH HAZARDS

• Dressing to thrill can make you ill!

Some types of sexy underwear and clothes can actually make the wearer ill – that's the warning that comes from Dr Teresa Woods, a Los Angeles physician, who said: "There's no doubt about it, lingerie that makes you feel sexy can also make you most unwell." This is why:
• Very tight-fitting underwear can interfere with blood circulation and could even cause life-threatening clots.
• A tight bra that sends shivers down your partner's spine could send painful spasms down yours, triggering headaches or neck pains.
• Skimpy panties may bring on yeast infection or skin rashes.
• Tight corsets can also: make women incontinent; cause varicose veins; or weaken stomach muscles.

"Many women suffer neck pains backaches and headaches from wearing seductive corsets and other tightly-fitting clothes, but they never realise the cause of their discomfort," said Dr Woods.

HEART DISEASE

• Forgive to live longer

As they say, to err is human, to forgive is divine. But now is seems that to forgive may also save you from a potentially fatal heart attack.

That's the implied message from a recent study which concluded that people who carry a grudge or who never let go of their anger have a significantly increased risk of heart attack and other heart disease.

During the study, patients were asked to undergo various psychological tests, all of which were aimed at increasing their stress levels. In the first test, the patients were faced with tough-to-solve mathematical problems; in another, they had to play-act and deliver a speech in which they defended themselves against an unfair and unfounded charge of shoplifting; and the third test required them to remember and describe in fulsome detail all the details of an occurrence that really got them extremely angry at the time.

And, it was this last test that really produced maximum bodily reaction sending the subjects' blood pressures sky high and even literally impairing the pumping action of their hearts.

Noting that of the three forms of stress forced upon the subjects that it was anger which had the greatest effect on the cardiovascular system, Dr C. Barr Taylor, a Stanford University professor of psychiatry who had helped conduct the experiments, concluded: "Obviously anyone suffering from heart problems should endeavour to reduce his or her level of anger, and that includes not holding a grudge. In fact, this advice should be followed by everyone."

This view was emphatically endorsed by Dr William Castelli, a top Harvard cardiologist, who added: "Carrying anger around with you for a long time can kill you."

• Forget the apple, make it an orange a day!

If you want to keep the cardiac surgeon away, then you should have an orange a day, according to a new university study.

"An orange a day would aid/prevent 'bad' cholesterol from clogging your arteries and help you avoid deadly heart disease," claimed Dr Ishwarhal Jialal, professor of internal medicine and clinical nutrition at the University of Texas, who explained that the effects of LDL cholesterol in causing fatty deposits and narrowing arteries can be combated by the vitamin C in an orange.

"My research shows that it takes just one daily dose of 60 milligrams of vitamin C to achieve this health benefit," he said, "and a convenient way to get this amount is from one medium-size orange or a small glass of orange juice." Dr Jialal explained that for most people sixty milligrams of vitamin C provided the maximum protection. so eating more than one orange a day wouldn't provide any extra help. "Diabetics and people under stress should, however, take double that amount because they usually have lower levels of vitamin C to start with," he added.

• Hot head can mean a bad heart

People who easily lose their temper are three times more likely to suffer heart attacks than those who always manage to stay as cool as a cucumber, researchers have discovered.

Scientists at Harvard University have confirmed that angry outbursts can actually trigger heart attacks, and that those most at risk are people with 'hostile personalities and cynical dispositions'.

Explained Dr James Muller, chief of cardiology at Harvard: "Angry outbursts can release blood clots that may block narrowed arteries and thereby choke off the supply of blood to a section of the heart muscle. The chances of a heart attack are increased three times during outbursts by susceptible men."

Dr Muller also warned that people who suddenly engaged in vigorous exercise – without having done so previously on a regular basis – were five times more likely to have a heart attack, but that there was no increased risk for those who exercised vigorously on a regular basis after having gradually worked up their fitness programme.

• How you relax may reveal HEART RISK

If you frequently relax by putting both your hands behind your head and leaning against the cradle formed by them, this could mean that you're possibly heading for heart problems.

Explains Dr Henry Landry, of Montreal, Canada: "This pose is a bit of body language that could indicate you have heart disease and don't know it. Of course, not all people who put their hands behind their heads have heart disease, but I have observed some close links."

Dr Landry says that the positioning of the hands in that way makes it easier for the heart to get oxygen. "People with an unsufficient supply of oxygen to the heart may unconsciously adopt this position so the heart doesn't have to pump so hard."

• Go to work to avoid a HEART ATTACK

Women who have jobs outside the home are less likely to suffer heart attacks than housewives.

That's the surprising finding of a study of 700 women by a team at the University of Texas Health Science Center, San Antonio, which found that women with jobs had lower levels of stress than their non-working counterparts. "Working women were also found to have significantly higher blood levels of high-density lipoproteins," explained Dr Helen Hazuda, one of the researchers. "High levels of lipoproteins, which carry a harmful form of cholesterol out of the bloodstream and the body, have been associated with a reduced risk of heart disease."

The study also showed that women who had outside jobs tended to be less fat than housewives, smoked less and took more exercise. "As a group, they also tended to drink more," added Dr Hazuda, "and alcohol – if taken in moderation – helps raise the level of lipoproteins."

HEARTBURN

• Easy tips to stop the pain of heartburn

The pain and misery of heartburn can be surprisingly easy to prevent, according to a leading expert.

"Simple precautionary measures are the best cure for nine out of ten of people who suffer heartburn," says Dr Donald Castell, who heads the Gastroenterology Department at Wake Forest University in Winston-Salem, N.C. These are his recommendations:
• Avoid wearing clothes that are tight around the waist or the stomach.

• Always eat slowly, taking small mouthfuls and chewing your food thoroughly.
• Change to a diet that is low in fat and high in protein.
• Lose weight if you're at all overweight. The pressure of extra weight in the abdomen can provoke heartburn more frequently.
• Avoid these foods: chocolate, coffee, alcohol, fizzy drinks, and very hot or highly seasoned dishes.
• Cultivate relaxation.
• Stop or reduce smoking.
• Avoid bending forward or stooping to lift heavy objects.
• Try eating smaller quantities of food during your main meals, supplementing these if necessary with smaller snacks.

Although most instances of heartburn are due to unjudicious eating habits, it can also be the result of other problems – such as a hiatus hernia – and sufferers are advised to consult their doctor if the symptoms are severe, persistent or regular.

HEPATITIS

• Drink may protect you from HEPATITIS A

It's a known fact that when a group of diners share a pile of oysters, some of them may get a hepatitis A infection while others get off scot-free. It's always been assumed that the victims were simply unlucky and got a 'bad' oyster and the others didn't.

A new study has, however, shed a different light on why some should escape infection. During an outbreak of hepatitis in Florida, researchers discovered that people who had taken 'strong drink' – that is, either wine or whisky in which the alcohol was at least 20% proof – were much less likely to become sick and that the chances of becoming affected were up to 9 per cent less if you boozed it up with your shell dinner.

Further research is now being planned to find out if alcohol's seemingly miraculous preventive powers may also apply to other kinds of infections.

HICCUPS

• Seven ways to cure HICCUPS

Hiccups are the result of an abrupt involuntary lowering of the diaphragm and closure of the sound-producing folds at the end of the trachea, this producing a characteristic sound as the breath is drawn in. Frequent hiccups need medical attention as they may be caused by indigestion or a more serious disorder.

For the occasional hiccup, there's a wealth of home spun remedies which could help:
• Hold a paper bag against the mouth and nose and breathe very hard into it for about a dozen times.
• Swallowing a teaspoonful of granulated sugar can modify the nervous impulses triggering off the diaphragm.
• Hold your breath for as long as reasonably possible and swallow

when you feel a hiccup coming on. This may interrupt the contractions.
• Fill a glass of water, bend over forward and drink the water upside down to stretch the diaphragm and stop the hiccups.
• Suck a lemon wedge soaked with Angostura bitters.
• Tickling the roof of the mouth with a clean cotton swab where the soft and hard palate meet may stop the spasms.
• Make up a poultice of half a teaspoonful of cayenne pepper to a pint of vinegar, thickened with corn meal, whole wheat flour or linseed meal. Apply the poultice to the diaphragm.

HONEY

• When honey is bad for infants

Babies less than a year old should never be given honey because it can lead to a condition known as infant botulism.

That's the warning from health authorities in California where during a three-month period, eight out of twenty reported cases of infant botulism were linked to eating honey. Symptoms of infant botulism include: constipation, lethargy and feeding problems.

HOPE

• Hope really does make a difference

"Hope is truly a medicine that can

literally mean the difference between life and death during a potentially fatal illness," says Dr Louis Gottschalk, a psychiatrist at the University of California at Irvine, who has devised a 'hope scale' that measures a patient's will to live and also suggests ways to renew and increase that hope.

In a study, he found that cancer patients who scored high in his test survived considerably longer after radiation treatment than those who had scored low.

HORMONES

• Fat keeps older women feeling sexy

Extra body fat can help keep women feeling sexy even after the menopause.

"Naturally-occuring hormones that stimulate female sexual desire are created in greater quantities if the body has more fat tissue," explained Dr Pentiti Siiteri, of UCLA, California. "However, extreme obesity can create too many hormones and increase the risk of some forms of cancer."

• New hope for women with ACNE or EXCESS HAIR

Women who suffer from acne or excess hair may be able to overcome these problems by simply taking the birth-control pill, say researchers.

Explained Dr Stewart Reingold, an assistant professor of paediatrics at the University of Chicago School of Medicine: "We've done an in-depth study of 61 women, aged 18 to 21, with acne or excessive hair growth and found that half of them had higher than normal levels of male hormones – and this is something that can be treated by taking the birth-control pill or other medications that reduce these hormones."

Dr Reingold's findings were endorsed by another survey conducted by Dr Emil Steinberger, professor of reproductive endocrinology at the University of Texas in Houston who said: "In a study of 140 women whose average age was 35 we found that 90 per cent of those with acne had elevated levels of testosterone. Acne or excessive hair are both dependent on male hormones and, if you're troubled by either of these, you should ask your doctor for help."

HOSPITALISATION

• A room with a view helps you get better quicker

Hospital patients who have a room with a view of trees recover more quickly than those who don't.

"Being able to look out on a pleasant outdoor scene appears to ease postoperative anxiety and improve several aspects of recovery," said Roger Ulrich, an associate professor at the University of Delaware, USA, after he had studied the recovery records of hundreds of patients at a local hospital.

"Compared to those whose window looked out on a wall, patients whose view included trees had shorter postoperative stays, fewer negative evaluations from nurses, needed fewer strong doses of painkillers and also had fewer postsurgical complications," he added. "I believe that the explanation for this is that when something holds your attention and elicits a positive feeling, it may have a blocking function to adverse things and as such offer a restorative or recuperative effect."

HOUSEWORK

- **Men who do housework are healthier**

If you're a married man and want to be healthier, then lend a hand with the housework – that's the message from a recent study which looked at 160 men over a period of four years and compared the illness rate of those who did housework with those who didn't.

Explained Dr John Gottman, professor of psychology at the University of Washington in America: "We measured colds, gastrointestinal troubles and every possible kind of medical problem and found that men who did housework were sick a lot less than men who did not."

As to why this should be so, Dr Gottman speculated that men who wash dishes, dust rooms and do laundry are "more involved with their spouses and are better able to handle marriage conflicts.

"On the other hand, the men who didn't do housework were more involved in other things such as their work," he added. "They were also more withdrawn from their marriages and suffered more from the effect of stress."

HUGGING

- **Why hugging makes you feel good**

Princess Diana's well-known views about the benefits of a good hug has found scientific endorsement from two experts in America.

"Hugging is a miracle medicine that can relieve many physical and emotional problems," declared Dr Isidore Ziferstein, a Los Angeles psychiatrist. "It's more than an expression of love - it triggers the release of chemicals in the brain that make people feel good and thereby helps combat depression and stress. And, since the body's immune system is strengthened by a positive attitude, hugging helps protect you against illness."

"Hugging can also raise tolerance to pain," added Dr David Bresler, a former director of the UCLA Pain Control Unit.

HYPERTENSION

- **Fingerprints provide HEART HEALTH clue**

The chances of you developing high blood pressure which can lead to heart disease can be detected by analysing your fingerprint patterns, according to recent research completed by the Medical Research Council's epidemiology unit which found that:

• 'Whorl' fingerprint patterns, as well as long hands or a narrow palm were all signs indicating that hypertension were likely.

• The more fingers had 'whorls', the greater the increase above normal blood pressure would be.

Based on the belief that susceptibility to hypertension begins in the womb, the study looked at 139 men and women born in the same hospital. As adults, 93 of them who had had whorls on one or more fingers at birth had higher blood pressure than the others whose fingers had other patterns, such as 'arches' or 'loops'.

A whorl pattern can be distinguished from the others because it is not as symmetrically concentric and includes a crescent-shaped island of ridges partially surrounding the central point.

IMPOTENCY

• Lover's guide to alcohol

Most of us are aware of the fact that having too much to drink can temporarily affect a man's ability to make love, but what is less known is that alcohol can also be detrimental to potency in the long-term.

New research indicates that alcohol decreases the body's ability to produce testosterone, creating in effect, a male menopause, decreasing the libido or sex drive and affecting sexual functions. There is an enzyme of testosterone known as dihydroxytestosterone, which is broken down by another body enzyme whose job it is to break down alcohol. When this enzyme goes to work on alcohol, it also breaks down the testosterone enzyme resulting in lower testosterone levels. At the same time this enzyme also stimulates the production of a hormone that causes an increase in feminising characteristics, such as enlarged breasts or shrunken testicles. Too much of this effect for too long a period of time can, of course, lead to major long-term problems and studies of chronic alcoholics have indicated that 80 per cent of them have radically decreased sex drives or are impotent.

Under normal circumstances, however, alcohol in small amounts can be helpful for lovers because it reduces anxiety, lowers inhibitions, and frees sexual response.

INCONTINENCE

• Don't allow your bladder to become lazy

The extent to which incontinence – a disorder that is estimated to trouble at least one in twenty people some time during their lives – can be prevented still remains largely a matter for conjecture as there are strong differences of opinion on this subject within the medical profession. There is, however, one very specific preventive measure that all experts agree can help and that is that you should avoid allowing your bladder to become 'lazy'.

And, the way to prevent this happening is remarkably easy, just don't fall into the habit of going to the toilet more frequently than necessary. If you're doing this more than, say, six or seven times a day and perhaps once during the night, see if you can reduce this frequency by just telling yourself to hang on a little bit longer. The reason for doing this is that a bladder that is 'pampered' by being emptied just as as soon as it sends out the slightest sign of being full is much more likely to eventually become a lazy one. What's more, you will also become more and more aware of the signals it sends and you will even possibly try to anticipate these, thereby further increasing the number of times you go to the toilet.

Experts say that a healthy bladder should ideally be allowed to fill to near capacity before it is emptied as draining it time and time again when it's only a quarter filled or so will in due course reduce its ability to hold a larger volume of liquid.

The other thing that you should do is to ensure that when you do empty your bladder you do so fully.

There are two main reasons for this: firstly, a bladder that is left partially drained with a permanent residue of urine is more likely to become infected; secondly, emptying it fully will make it easier for you to empty it less frequently. Conversely, it has also been shown that if you empty it less frequently, it will eventually become easier to empty it fully.

• Five dangerous fallacies about incontinence

Urinary incontinence affects many people as they become older. And, while the problem can often easily be solved by some very simple exercises, the sad fact is that many people don't seek help from their doctors. One of the reasons for this is that many believe in various myths about their condition and give up the battle against incontinence before it's even begun. Here are some of the fallacies:

• **Fallacy Number One:** Incontinence is just something we have to put up with as we get older. It's a natural part of the body deteriorating. The truth: Incontinence is certainly not an inevitable part of advancing years and should it occur, it can usually be reversed easily.

• **Fallacy Number Two:** Incontinence is irreversible. Once you've got it, you're stuck with it. The truth: This is perhaps the greatest fallacy of all because nearly all cases of incontinence can be treated successfully.

• **Fallacy Number Three:** Women who have had children must expect to suffer some incontinence. The truth: It's a fact that the strain of giving birth can damage the muscles that support the bladder and some loss of control may follow temporarily. But this control can invariably be restored, usually simply with some exercises.

• **Fallacy Number Four:** The problem will go away of its own accord as my body will heal itself. The truth: With rare exceptions, this is not likely to happen unless you take positive steps to do something about it. The chances for a full and comparatively quick restoration of bladder control are all the greater the sooner you tackle the problem.

• **Fallacy Number Five:** My mother and her mother too were also troubled by incontinence. I guess it's just hereditary. The truth: There is no solid evidence to give credence to the idea that incontinence is hereditary.

So if you're having the least problem with bladder control, don't let misconceptions stop you from seeking the help that is readily available from your doctor and which almost certainly will bring about a complete cure.

INFECTION RISKS

• **Hot air hand dryers breed GERMS**

The country's washrooms have been turned into hotbeds of germs since the widespread introduction of hot air hand dryers – that's the finding of a special survey carried out by the University of Westminster.

Although the machines are claimed to be more hygienic than other drying methods, their use in fact creates a 500 per cent increase of germs on the hands, claim researchers. What's more, many people end up finishing their drying by rubbing their hands on their clothing or hair. "Men are more likely to do this than women and often use the seat of their trousers," said one researcher, "and this could increase the chances of bacterial transmission."

According to the survey, the most hygienic drying method was paper towels, as the use of these actually reduced bacteria on the hands.

INFERTILITY

• **Vitamin boosts male fertility**

Just taking extra vitamin C may well be enough to solve the problems of the millions of men suffering from a very common type of infertility known as 'sperm-clumping'. Research at the University of Texas has found that the vitamin is almost 100 per cent effective in reversing this form of infertility which is believed to affect about one in six men over the age of 25.

"The vitamin makes the sperm more mobile and by doing so dramatically increases the man's chances of fertilising the woman's egg and making her pregnant," explained Dr E. B. Dawson, who conducted several studies to confirm the vitamin's efficacy. "This is a safe, easy, inexpensive way to significantly improve the chances of a couple suffering from infertility because of sperm-clumping. It means that these men's wives don't have to resort to artificial insemination to have their own children."

Proof of vitamin C's power to overcome sperm-clumping was overwhelmingly demonstrated by one study in which 27 men with the problem were divided into two groups. Twenty of them were given an extra 1,000 milligrams of vitamin C for sixty days and the other seven received no supplements.

"All of the 20 men who had extra vitamin C got their wives pregnant, and none of the seven in the other group did, reported Dr Dawson.

In a similar study, 30 young men were split into three groups. One group received 1,000 milligrams of vitamin C daily for a month; the second group received only one fifth of that amount; and the last group were given a placebo pill.

"Sperm-clumping was dramatically reduced for those who had the full dosage of additional vitamin C," said Dr Dawson. "The smaller dose was almost as effective. But there was no significant change for the men who had received the placebo."

Dr Dawson's findings were endorsed by Dr William McGanity, professor of obstetrics and gynaecology at the same university, who stated: "I agree that taking 1,000 milligrams of vitamin C daily for a month reduces sperm-clumping and boosts fertility. My own feeling is that you can probably also do this with a dosage level as low as 250 milligrams daily."

INTELLIGENCE

• Being the first born doesn't mean you're smarter

Two Swiss psychiatrists say that they have fully disproven the widely held belief that first-born children are smarter and more likely to succeed than their siblings.

Cecile Ernst and Jules Angst, both of the University of Zurich, reached that conclusion after studying some 1,500 individuals and, according to them, the effect of birth order upon intelligence "falls somewhere between negligible and non-existent".

Despite these new findings, many experts are still convinced that a first-born child has a better chance to attain his or her intelligence potential because, as stated in the famous paper by R. B. Zagone, of the University of Michigan, "each new child decreases the intellectual environment of the home".

Stress reduces children's IQs

Children who are brought up in a family environment that is

frequently stressful are more likely to develop lower intelligence quotients than average.

Dr Bernard Brown, of Georgetown University in Washington, has just completed a massive survey and he says the results clearly show that children's IQs drop dramatically when family levels of stress are high. "The extent of the drop varies considerably, but my research has discovered that stress can easily account for a drop from an above average score of 105 to a below average rating of only 91," he said.

JET LAG

• Sleeping pill beats JET LAG

You can effectively treat jet lag with a short-acting sleeping pill, according to researchers at the world famous Stanford University Sleep Center in California.

Doctors found that the sleep medication triazolam completely reverses the daytime sluggishness and night-time insomnia associated with long-distance air travel.

Other new research suggests that jet lag will eventually be overcome by controlled injections of extra Melatonin, a hormone normally produced by the pineal gland.

JOGGING

• The risks of jogging

While most of us know that it can be dangerous to embark on too energetic a jogging programme, the actual odds on physically injuring yourself while doing so aren't all that good either, according to a recent American study which revealed:

• One in three joggers can expect to sustain a running-related injury a year.

• Half of these injuries will be in the knee or the foot.

Somewhat better are the chances of avoiding other accidents as it has been calculated that an average jogger logging 10 to 19 miles a week is likely to be struck by an object thrown from a car once every 12 years, bitten by a dog once every 26 years, and hit by a car every 135 years.

• Skipping is better than jogging

The childhood pastime of skipping is better exercise for you than jogging, according to Dr Irving Dardik, past chairman and founder of the US Olympic Committee Sports Medicine Committee.

"In fact, you'd be foolish to jog," he added, "because it causes so many unnecessary injuries."

Dr Dardik said he became sold on the benefits of skipping after studying its effects on Olympic hurdlers, shot-putters and high jumpers. "It proved itself to be an excellent cardiovascular exercise and was far less hard on the body than jogging," he said. "For instance, when you jog, each foot absorbs up to five times your body weight from the force of the impact when it strikes the ground and this can damage your feet, ankles, hips and knees. On the other hand, when you skip, the shock of hitting the ground is absorbed by both feet, reducing the stress on your bones and muscles."

Dr Dardik's view is endorsed by Dr William Castelli, director of the famed Framingham Heart Study, who said: "Skipping is great exercise that can give you all the benefits of jogging at a lower risk to your knees, ankles and hips."

KISSING

• Kissing dental cavities goodbye

Kissing can help prevent cavities, says a dentist, because it stimulates the salivary glands, and the extra saliva assists in rinsing food particles off the teeth.

"Saliva also lowers the acid level in the mouth," added Dr Sam Green, director of community dentistry for the Etobicoke Health Department in Ontario, Canada. "And, because cavities need an acidic base in which to form, the increase in the flow of saliva is helpful in that area as well."

• Mother can kiss away pain

A mother's kiss can cure a child's pain almost every time – and will usually do so ten times faster than even morphine.

That's the surprising conclusion of a study by Professor Athanasies Prosalentis, of Athens, Greece, who recorded the effects of various painkillers on hundreds of ailing children. "Whatever the cause of the pain may be, a mother's kiss will almost invariably ease it," he said. "And, of course, that treatment is also free of any possible side-effects."

KNUCKLES

• The truth about knuckle cracking

The old wives' tale that says that knuckle cracking causes arthritis has been fully debunked by the results of a new study.

"We couldn't find any evidence associating knuckle cracking with osteoarthritis," concluded Dr David Axelrod, an associate professor of medicine at the Medical College of Ohio, USA, after a survey of 300 subjects, all of whom were at least 45 years old, the age after which arthritic disease tends to show up in most cases.

The study looked at 74 people who were 'frequent and chronic', knuckle crackers and 226 people who weren't and revealed that the incidence of arthritis between the two groups was the same. "However, we did find that habitual knuckle crackers were more likely to suffer occasional hand swelling and sometimes the loss of strength in their grip," added Dr Axelrod.

LEFT-FACED

• Is your child left-faced?

If your child is left-faced, the chances are high that he or she could become a talented musician, composer or singer, says a noted American psychologist.

Dr Karl Smith, formerly of the University of Wisconsin at Milwaukee, says that if the left side of the face is dominant that indicates tremendous musical potential. "Beethoven, Brahms, Lizt and Wagner were all left-faced," he points out, "and so were 98 of the opera stars I studied."

How to tell if someone is left-faced? People who are, have lower brows, more pronounced dimples and wrinkles on the left side which is also the more expressive one.

LEG CRAMPS

• Four ways to beat LEG CRAMPS

Cramps in the leg are usually due to fatigue, imperfect posture, or stress, but may also be caused by an imbalance of salts in the body. In some instances, cramp may be avoided by taking extra nutrients and those which have been found most helpful are:

• **Calcium.** Supplementing your diet with about 900 mg of calcium daily may reduce the incidence of cramps.

• **Vitamin E.** Taking an extra 100 IUs of vitamin E with each meal could also help.

• **Magnesium.** Some chronic sufferers from leg cramps were found to be deficient in magnesium. You can increase your intake of this mineral by eating more beans, nuts, bananas, potatoes, whole wheat and soya products.

• **Potassium.** Another vital mineral which can help. Rich sources of potassium include fish, tomatoes, raisins, milk, orange juice, bananas and potatoes. If the cramps persist, you should see your doctor and you should also get their advice before taking extra vitamins or minerals.

LONGEVITY

• Good health habits

You may be able to add up to 15 years to your lifespan by obeying the Ten Commandments of Health which have been formulated by two top health experts.

One of these, Dr George Mann, associate professor of medicine and biochemistry at Vanderbilt University School of Medicine in the USA, said: "We can all live longer, happier, healthier and more satisfying lives by following this plan."

Added Dr William Castelli, medical director of the world famous Framingham Heart Study: "By adopting these good health habits you could add 10 or 15 years to your life."

Here are their Ten Commandments of Health:

1) Thou shalt be physically active. "The right kind of exercise is the first essential for a healthy life," said Dr Mann.

2) Thou shalt drink water when exercising. "And, you should not leave taking in water until you feel thirsty, as by this time your body will already have become partially dehydrated," he added.

3) Thou shalt eat a variety of foods each day. "And, in particular remember the importance of eating fresh fruit and vegetables daily," Dr Mann stressed.

4) Thou shalt avoid animal fat. "And, this includes not only fat on meat, but also butter and lard," Dr Castelli pointed out.

5) Thou shalt eat only one main meal a day. "This applies only, however, to those who like most of us lead sedentary lives, burning up but few calories," Dr Mann added.

6) Thou shalt eat seafood at least two or three times a week. "Seafood contains substances that greatly reduce the risk of blood clots," Dr Mann explained.

7) Thou shalt not eat red meat more than two or three times a week. "Although red meat is an excellent source of protein and iron, too much of it will harm you," stated Dr Castelli.

8) Thou shalt be careful with alcohol. "If you must drink, be sure you do so in moderation," said Dr Mann.

9) Thou shalt avoid phosphates and seek out calcium. "Too much phosphate and too little calcium can lead to brittle bones," Dr Mann asserted. "Drink at least a glass of milk a day to boost your calcium level."

10) Thou shalt shun sodium and pursue potassium. "Salt is a major contributor to hypertension and heart disease," said Dr Castelli. "Eating several pieces of fruit every day is a very good way to maintain your potassium level which is essential to control blood pressure," added Dr Mann.

• Your waist and hips predict how long you'll live

If you're over the age of fifty-five and your waist measurement is the same or more than that of your hips, your chances of dying within the next five years are substantially higher than that of someone whose waist is narrower than their hips.

That's the finding that emerged from a recent study of 41,837 Iowa residents, aged 55 to 69 years. This survey supported similar conclusions reached after a study by researchers at the University of Minnesota School of Public Health.

Apparently, what really matters is not how much you weigh, but where on your body that extra weight is carried and this can be summed up as 'apple-shaped is bad, pear-shaped is good'.

The Minnesota survey found that lean men and women whose waists were bigger than their hips faced the greatest risk of death – and these findings applied equally whether the subjects smoked or not.

"For women, the waist-to-hip ratio should be less than 0.8," explained Dr Aaron R. Folsom, one of the leaders of the study. "That is, the waist should be less than 80 per cent of the hips. To calculate the ratio, divide the waist circumference by the hip circumference. For example, a woman with 40-inch hips should have a waist no larger than 32 inches.

"The ratio is more forgiving for men, but it should still be less than 0.95," he added. "This means that the waist has only to be slightly, smaller than the hips, only slightly but definitely smaller nevertheless."

In the Iowa study it was found that the risk of death for a woman with 40-inch hips increased by a massive 60 per cent with every six-inch increase in her waist.

Neither of the two teams of researchers were able to offer any explanation as to why people with midriffs larger than their waists were so much more likely to die sooner. "We don't know if this is cause-and-effect or if there is some underlying abnormality," said Dr Folsom. "The hip-to-waist ratio may just be a marker for some other process."

Of course, a high-body mass – that's when one is too heavy for one's height – has been used for years as a good predictor of early mortality. But, say the researchers, the waist-to-hip ratio is even

more consistently reliable as a measurement tool.

LUNG CANCER

• Direct cobalt treatment cuts RADIATION RISKS

Lung cancer can now be treated with radioactive cobalt pellets which are placed directly on malignancies without causing harm to surrounding healthy tissues.

"This is an excellent way of treating those patients who have had all the external radiation therapy they can stand," said Dr James Harrell, a leading cancer specialist at the Medical Center at the University of Chicago in San Diego. "It increases survival, and improves the quality of life."

The pellets are delivered to the tumour sites through a special tube as the surgeon controls the procedure by watching it through a bronchoscope. The tube goes in through one nostril, and the bronchoscope through the other.

MAGNESIUM

• EXERCISE can deprive you of magnesium

Strenuous exercise may deplete the body of the essential mineral magnesium, according to research recently completed in America.

Previous studies had indicated that if you deprive a muscle of magnesium it can't contract properly. People who drink too much alcohol and diabetics are particularly prone to be low in magnesium, but, add the researchers, it would seem that many others generally thought to be healthy are also not getting enough of this vital mineral.

MARRIAGE

• Your spouse can be dangerous to your health

WARNING: Marriage can create real health hazards, according to a group of prominent doctors.

The message that you should be aware of, as well as the effects your spouse can have on your state of health comes from physicians at the Oregon Health Sciences University in Portland, USA, and is the result of a study of 201 couples ranging in age from the early twenties to the mid-fifties.

"If a wife is a heavy eater, her husband is likely to overstuff himself as well; and if a man drinks too much, his wife is also likely to do the same," said Dr Jack Hollis, who reported the conclusions of the study at the annual meeting of the American Heart Association, adding that "there's no doubt that peer pressure in the home plays a big part in what happens there.

"If a doctor, for instance, finds that the husband is in danger from high blood pressure from eating too many fatty foods, then instead of just telling him to cut down on his fat intake, he should also ask the wife to help by setting a good example. After all, it's for the good of both of them. The same goes for smoking. If a doctor wants the husband to cut down, he should ask the wife to cut down also."

The study looked at how marriage partners influenced each other in the use of cigarettes, alcohol, coffee, as well as so called 'recreational drugs' like marijuana. These were the key findings:

Cigarettes: If their wives are smokers, then the men are 2.6 times more likely to smoke as well when compared to men whose wives don't smoke. Wives of smoking husbands are 2.9 times more likely to also smoke than women married to non-smokers.

Alcohol: The chances that husbands are drinkers are one and a half times greater if they're married to women who drink. Women whose husbands drink are nearly twice as likely to be drinkers themselves compared to those with non-drinking husbands.

Coffee: The study looked at those couples who drank what was considered to be a 'large' amount of coffee, this being defined as four cups a day or more. Once again, the chances of wives or husbands over-indulging in the brew were about twice as likely if their partners did the same.

Marijuana: The effect of 'peer pressure' within marriage was startling in this connection. If the woman smoked, the chances of the husband doing the same were 6.2 higher than if she didn't. And, a woman married to a marijuana user was 8.8 times more likely to do so herself.

As might be expected, the example set by their partner also greatly influenced eating habits of both men and women. If the husband's diet was high in cholesterol-laden fatty meats there was a three in four chance that the wife's was just as high. The same likelihood applied to husbands whose wives had a high cholesterol intake.

The spouses of subjects who were overweight were also more likely to be so. If his wife was more than 20 pounds overweight, there was a 70 per cent chance that the husband was as well. Women married to overweight men were also overweight three times out of four.

Strangely enough, the survey found that when it came to exercising or taking prescribed drugs, the marriage partners had virtually no influence upon each other's habits, although men as a whole were more likely to exercise than their wives.

• Why men cheat on their mates

Men cheat on their mates because the male sex drive is so powerful that they just can't help themselves and not because they want to.

That's the finding of anthropologist Dr Helen Fisher, an American expert on marriage and divorce, who explained: "Men are driven by an underlying restlessness, a biological force that spurs half of all men to stray at times. Cheating is part of our ancient reproductive game."

Some of Dr Fisher's other findings include:
• Falling in love can truly make you euphoric and giddy as our emotions cause our bodies to produce natural amphetamines in the brain.
• Love at first sight is usually the product of unusually high hormonal levels.
• Both men and women really do fall harder when the intended object of their affection plays hard to get.

• Forget the seven year itch – it happens after four years

"If they're going to break up at all, most modern marriages will do so after four years," said New York researcher Dr Helen Fisher. "And, the four year period is interesting," she adds, "because that is exactly the length of time that man a million years ago spent with a particular mate to raise their young before straying to father more heirs elsewhere." Marital break-up, of course, also often triggers off health problems and scores extremely highly on all standard stress inventories used by psychologists.

• Separate bedrooms can save marriages

Sleeping apart can actually save your marriage from falling apart.

That's the surprising advice offered by Dr Laura Singer, a

marriage counsellor and past president of the American Association for Marriage and Family Therapy, who explained: "We're usually loath to have separate bedrooms because of the emphasis that's put on togetherness and we might also be concerned that others might snicker. These are, however, bad reasons for avoiding separate bedrooms when this step could solve simple problems that otherwise can destroy marriages."

For example, Dr Singer explained: "If your spouse is a loud and irritating snorer or often stays up late reading or watching TV, these actions can not only keep you awake, but eventually make you deeply resentful.

"Harbouring this resentment can eventually ruin your marriage, but sleeping in separate bedrooms would have nipped all those bad feelings in the bud."

Dr Singer added that you shouldn't try separate bedrooms until you had first experimented with separate beds. "And, if that doesn't work," she said, "here's how to sleep apart without hurting your partner's feelings . . ."

1) Make sure that you convince your partner that sleeping separately is a good idea before you start.

2) Also make sure that your choice of separate bedrooms or beds is made for good rational reasons, not out of anger or spite.

3) Make plans with your partner for specific times when you can be together and make love.

"You have to be sure that the needs of both are fully met," she concluded. "If they are, then sleeping apart can actually strengthen your marriage and in turn lead to a lasting relationship."

• It takes more than drugs to cure 'marriage migraine'

Marriage can be a real headache, according to medical researchers – and it's one that takes more than analgesics to shift.

A study recently completed at the University of Washington School of Medicine, in Seattle, USA, found that people suffering from migraine were often involved in stressful marriages.

"It's my opinion that many of these have migraines to give expression to marital conflicts or stressful relationships they can't express in any other way," said Dr Bernard Beitman, the psychiatrist who led the study, which over two years investigated 40 married and single patients, all of whom had daily migraines. "Twelve of the seventeen single patients received relief when prescribed medication, but this only worked for four of the twenty-three who were married."

"We found that the married patients whose symptoms were not relieved by drugs either refused to admit they had a marital problem or simply blamed the other partner for their stress," he concluded.

MORNING SICKNESS

• Morning sickness protects the unborn

The morning sickness that accompanies many pregnancies may be nature's way of protecting the foetus during its first three months.

That's the theory that has been put forward by Margie Profet, a biologist at the University of California at Berkeley, after she found that the foods that most frequently make pregnant women nauseous are also the same ones that are often potentially the most dangerous to the foetus. Foods in this category include: vegetables with very strong smells, meat that is fried or grilled or slightly spoiled.

MOTORING

• Car seats are a pain

People who spend more than half of their working day driving are three times more likely to suffer a slipped disc, says Mark Porter, of Loughborough University, who has made a special study of the subject. "And, these people also have a 16 per cent higher incidence of lower back pain," he added.

Commented the National Back Pain Association: "Most car seats are very badly designed and that's

why drivers have so many back pain problems."

MUSIC

• Music can be bad for your eyes

Your eyesight can be adversely affected by music that's too loud.

According to American Family Physician Magazine, college students were asked to listen to music at a comfortable level, then at a high level. Eighty per cent of the students tested showed a decrease in their ability to see well while listening to the louder music.

• You'll recover faster with music

Music can not only relieve pain but it can also speed up your recovery, say top experts.

• Drugs were unable to control the pains of a cancer patient, reported the Canadian Medical Association Journal. But soothing music "caused her to relax and her respiration to deepen until she fell into a deep sleep".

• "Listening to music accelerates recovery time from surgery," declared Dr James McCarron, chief of surgery at Jefferson General Hospital, Port Townsend, Washington.

• "Soothing music in the coronary unit promotes rest, this, in turn, reduces elevated blood pressure and heart rate as well as relieving pain by increasing tolerance to it," said Dr Raymond Bahr, of St Agnes Hospital in Baltimore, Maryland.

The role of music – or rather the speed of its beat which is correctly known as its 'tempo' – in controlling heart beat rate is, of course, well established and is used in all sorts of therapies.

MYTHS

• Twelve myths about your body

You may love it or loathe it, but one thing is for sure, you have to live with your body. It is therefore important to understand how it works and to do that here are twelve myths you'll have to shrug off:

1) We have five senses. In fact, scientists have identified at least 120 separate senses which, apart from sight, hearing, taste, smell and touch, include: senses of movement, balance and position, as well as internal senses that tell us when we're hungry, thirsty or have other needs. Touch itself is three separate senses, reacting to temperature, pressure and pain.

2) A tongue with a white coating means you're sick or constipated. Maybe so, but it's also normal to have a whitish, furry tongue if you smoke, often eat soft foods or even sleep with your mouth open.

3) An apple a day keeps the doctor away. By no means so and unless it's a hard apple that stimulates the flow of saliva, the acid in the fruit may even damage your teeth.

4) Extra vitamins are good for you. Our bodies can only handle a limited amount of vitamins. Surplus vitamin C probably won't harm you, but too much vitamin A – rich sources of which are dairy produce, vegetables and offal – or vitamin D – which abounds in cod liver oil and butter – can make you seriously unwell.

5) Aerobic exercise is better for you than ordinary exercise. Any exercise that makes you puff is 'aerobic' because that word simply means 'with oxygen'.

6) You'll see better in the dark if you eat lots of carrots. We need vitamin A (which is found in carrots) to see in dim light, but get all of it we need in a normal diet.

7) Feed a cold and starve a fever. You may need carbohydrates to make up for the calories lost by the sweating that could accompany either condition. Overeating won't speed a cold on its way and will just make you fat.

8) Fish feeds the brain and makes it more efficient. Yes, fish does feed the brain – but no more than any other part of your body!

9) Spinach will make you stronger. Spinach has had an undeserved good press because a scientist once put the decimal point in the wrong place and spinach only contains one tenth of the iron it was once thought to have. Gram for gram, meat will give ten times more

iron than spinach.

10) Sitting on a warm radiator gives you haemorrhoids. No, the main causes of haemorrhoids are hereditary weakness, strain, constipation and pregnancy.

11) You can ruin your sight with too much reading. The worst that can happen is that you'll strain the muscles around your eyes.

12) Men who wear hats are more likely to go bald. The main cause of baldness is heredity.

NAILS

• **Simple trick stops nail-biting**
You can kick the nail-biting habit with a simple psychological trick – when the urge to bite strikes, just clench your fist tightly for three minutes or so.

The technique worked wonders for hardened nail-biters during a study at Manchester Metropolitan University when three methods were compared. One group simply recorded their biting habits in a diary; a second group painted a bitter-tasting substance on their nails twice a day; the last group practised the fist-clenching technique and, at the end of four weeks, had nails that were significantly longer than the other two groups.

• **How to care for BRITTLE NAILS**
Here are some quick tips to help you deal with fingernails that have

become brittle:

• Put a drop of white iodine, which is available from most pharmacies, on dry, clean nails every night for a week, and once a week after that, to restore their strength.

• Try to use fingernail polish remover as little as possible.

• Avoid contact with detergents and chemicals by wearing gloves while washing up.

• Extra iron in your diet may also help. Foods rich in iron include: fish, whole grains, pulses, and dark green, leafy vegetables.

NASAL CONGESTION

• **How to keep your nose unclogged**
Nasal congestion is a frequent wintertime complaint and this occurs when the blood vessels in the nose enlarge and take up more space in the nasal cavity. As a result, the amount of air allowed in for breathing becomes restricted. There are two easy home remedies which can help relieve congestion:

1) The hot soup solution. A study has shown that many people find that drinking hot soup aids the flow of mucus and unclogs the nose. Adding onions or cayenne pepper to the soup may make it even more efficacious.

2) The eucalyptus cure. Place several eucalyptus leaves in a pan of boiling water for about five minutes. Turn off the heat and, with a towel draped around your head to

make a tent, lean over the pan and breathe in the herbal vapours, taking great care not to burn or scald yourself.

By the way, be sparing in the use of medicated nasal sprays, drops and inhalers. These work by shrinking swollen blood vessels in the nose and over-use of the decongestants can 'tire' these vessels and actually make congestion worse over a period of time.

• Pepper spray for nasal stuffiness

A new spray currently being tested with promising results at an allergy centre in Baltimore, Maryland, USA, uses capsaicin – the active ingredient in hot peppers – to relieve the symptoms of chronic nasal stuffiness. Eating red peppers, of course, has been for years a traditional folk remedy for easing a stuffy nose.

NAUSEA

• Spice can prevent NAUSEA

A common kitchen spice can help prevent the occurrence of nausea which frequently follows anaesthesia during surgery, according to a study at St Bartholomew's Hospital, London where patients given powdered ginger before surgery were only half as likely to experience nausea as compared with patients who didn't get the spice.

Normally, about one in three patients have significant nausea and/or vomiting after general anaesthesia. While there are drugs to combat this, these too can have undesirable side-effects.

"Ginger has no side-effects and it appears to work by absorbing toxins and acids as well as blocking gastrointestinal reactions connected to nausea," commented Dr Varro Tyler, a professor of pharmacology at Purdue University in the USA, commenting on the British results, who added: "I recommend that patients due to undergo surgery should ask their doctors if they should take a 500 milligram capsule of ginger compound an hour or so beforehand."

NIGHT SWEATS

• How to ease night sweats

Although primarily known as one of the more common short-term symptoms associated with the menopause, night sweats may be experienced by almost anyone at any time. Whether the basic cause of night sweats is hormonal or not, there are several practical things you can do to lessen the misery that accompanies it:

• Use bedsheets made from cotton as these will absorb the moisture better.

• If your bedroom is on the cool side and you need bedclothes for warmth, then use several thin layers rather than one thick one. That way, should you have a night sweat, you can shed some of the layers while still retaining enough warmth to stop you from shivering.

• If you're woken by a night sweat, don't panic. Try to relax, perhaps read or listen to the radio for a while, without allowing yourself to worry about the sleep you're missing.

• Avoid taking stimulants – and this includes coffee, tea, and cigarettes – shortly before going to bed as it has been found that these can contribute to the incidence of night sweats.

• Some people say that having a drink of water shortly before bedtime reduces the likelihood of night sweats. Other have claimed that keeping a window open has also helped.

Sweating is, of course, the natural way for the body to restore its natural temperature. Night sweats, however, occur when there seems to be no need for the body to lower its temperature and are believed to be the result of faulty or incorrect signals received by the sweat glands, this in the case of menopausal women being the result of changing hormonal levels affecting the performance of the hypothalamus which controls body temperature by dilating or constricting blood vessels.

Under normal circumstances, a person starts to sweat, depending on the clothing worn and activity engaged in, to reduce body temperature when the external temperature is above the range of 29 to 31 degrees Centigrade. Below this range, vasodilation is usually sufficient to keep the body cool enough. However, when the temperature of the blood reaching the hypothalamus is between one to one and a half degrees above 'normal' – for whatever reason this might have happened – nerve impulses will be sent from it to stimulate the sweat glands into action. These glands will then draw fluid from the blood and pass this through minute ducts onto the surface of the skin. As the sweat evaporates into the air it takes with it latent heat from the body and thereby reduces the internal temperature.

By the way, sweat evaporation for temperature control is mainly from the forehead, neck, upper lip, face and trunk, while sweating from the armpits, soles and palms seems to be more dependent upon emotional stress or other psychological factors than on the needs of internal temperature control.

NOISE POLLUTION

• Noise can be a real killer

Noise can be more than just a nuisance – it can easily make you sick and even kill you.

So says Dr Paul Lambert, of the University of Virginia Medical Center, who explained: "Noise affects the cardiovascular system, increasing both heart rate and blood pressure as well as releasing extra stress hormones. And, the stress caused by exposure to high levels of noise leads to constriction of blood vessels, a common symptom of heart disease." Even after the noise stops, the pulse rate and blood pressure remain high for some time, he added. Other surveys have also shown noise to trigger headaches, asthma, ulcers and colitis.

Additionally, noise causes mental stress as proven by studies in England and Los Angeles which showed that people living near airports were more prone to nervous breakdowns.

NOSE

• Your tell-tale nose

What your nose looks like is one of the best visible indicators of the state of health of the rest of your body.

"It's absolutely true," asserts Dr Robert S. Mendelsohn, a former associate professor of preventive medicine at the University of Illinois. "The condition of your nose can tell you how well the heart, stomach and many other internal organs are functioning.

This claim that the 'nose knows' is endorsed by Dr Keith Block, an expert in the art of 'visual diagnosis' who offered the following observations:
• If the tip of your nose is swollen, this may indicate that your heart may also be swollen or enlarged.
• Should the tip of your nose be

very hard, this might mean hardening of the arteries, high cholesterol and fatty deposits near the heart.
• An elongated vertical dimple or indentation in the centre of the nose could be the warning signal of an irregular heartbeat.
• Otherwise unexplained bumps on the nose may mean pancreas or kidney problems.

"What's more, a crooked nose can indicate which one of your parents' physical traits are most pronounced in you," added Dr Block. "A nose that slants to the right can signify that the mother's constitution is dominant while a nose that slants to the left is indicative that the father's constitution is dominant.

"A large nose is the sign of a strong constitution – while a small nose may mean a generally weaker one," he said.

Some other 'nose diagnostics':
• Red noses may be a sign of heart and circulatory troubles.
• A slight discoloration – with a brown, blue or black hue – may mean that you're likely to have spleen or pancreas problems.

NOSE, RUNNY

• Stopping a runny nose

If you've got a runny nose, but it's not bad enough to merit medical attention, you might care to try the following folk remedy: Add two or three drops of Tabasco sauce to a glass of water and drink it. In many instances, this will bring relief within minutes.

• Laser technique cures chronic RUNNY NOSES

A new laser technique takes only 15 minutes to cure people who suffer from chronic runny noses, leaving 85 per cent of those treated completely symptom free afterwards.

Chronic rhinitis, as the condition is called, happens when bony plates inside the nostrils swell and thereby interfere with the normal drainage from the sinuses. The new procedure deals with the problem by firing a laser burst through the nostrils at the plates thereby causing a layer of scar tissue to form. This scar tissue acts as a 'belt' around the plates, keeping them in check and stopping them from swelling.

The technique was developed by Dr Howard Levine, director of the Mount Sinai Nasal Sinus Center in Cleveland, who has used it so far on more than 200 patients with more than three quarters of them being fully cured.

OBESITY

• An extra good reason not to be overweight

Apart from all the well-known ones, there's now another good reason why it pays to keep your weight down because it has been found that overweight people may have unusually high levels of toxic chemicals stored in their fat tissues.

"Research has confirmed that DDT and other potent pesticides accumulate in fat deposits," said Dr George Blackburn, a nutrition expert at Harvard Medical School in America. "And, the greater the amount of fat tissue in the body, the greater the potential for these toxins to collect and persist in the system for long periods of time.

"Additionally, there is another danger when overweight people go on rapid weight-loss diets because metabolising too much fat too quickly can increase the risk of toxicity," he added, citing one case where a person became seriously ill when large amounts of DDT were released into his blood stream when he lost weight quickly.

• Overeating may be due to chemical defect

People who habitually overeat may do so because of a chemical defect in their body, say researchers at Thomas Jefferson University in Philadelphia.

"We have looked at hundreds of obese people and found evidence that many of them appeared to be suffering from a condition that actually stopped them from being able to readily sense when their stomachs were full," explained Dr Steven Peikin, who headed the project. "So far, we have been unable to fully identify the mechanism at work, but we think that it may be a chemical defect or deficiency of some sort."

Take your walk first, then eat! Forget the idea of walking off the calories after a meal – it's far better to take your stroll before you sit down to dine.

That's the message form the British Heart Foundation which reported that tests had shown that people who took a walk before ingesting a meal high in fats registered up to one third less fat in their blood afterwards than those who did not.

"There's no doubt about it – walking before a meal speeds up the breakdown of fat," said a spokesman for the foundation. "And that, of course, helps avoid heart disease."

ONIONS

• Onions can prevent STROKES and HEART ATTACKS

The common onion can be a powerful ally in the fight against heart attacks and strokes, says a leading American physician who prescribes an onion a day for his patients.

Dr Victor Gurewich, professor of medicine at Tufts University in Medford, Mass., says that the onions help clear the blood of fats and cholesterol that can block arteries thereby increasing the risk of heart problems.

"The onions work by increasing the production of the body's so-called 'good' cholesterol – the high density lipoprotein (HDL) – which keeps the blood flowing smoothly," he explained, adding that he has found that patients eating enough onions raised their HDL levels by an average of 30 per cent.

Although Dr Gurewich hasn't been able so far to isolate what ingredient in onions does the trick, he has found that the hotter the onion, the greater the effect.

OPERATIONS

• Replay your own EYE OPERATION

"Let me show you the video of my eye operation," iş an invitation that can be made by patients of a promotion conscious ophthalmologist.

Dr Norman Peterson, of Laguna Hills, California, makes video tapes of all his eye operations and gives them free to his patients because, he says, "it's a great promotion and it also takes the mystery out of the operation, showing the patients the fantastic progress of operative techniques".

ORAL CANCER

• Should it be a carrot a day?

Vitamin A and beta-carotene, the active ingredients in carrots, may help to guard against oral cancer, say scientists, who reported that the compounds were found to sharply reduce precancerous cells in the mouths of Filipino peasants who chew quids made from betel-nuts and tobacco. Quid chewing is blamed for several hundreds of thousands of deaths from oral cancer in Asia yearly.

OVARIAN CANCER

- **New test to detect OVARIAN CANCER**

Two new tests have been devised which will make it easier for ovarian cancer to be detected at an early stage when it can still be cured by surgery.

"The tests – involving blood samples and ultrasound probes – are expected to make general screening possible for the first time," said Professor William Collins, who has been coordinating the research at King's College Hospital, London.

Ovarian cancer currently affects 5,000 women a year and about 75 per cent of them die from the disease because it wasn't detected until it was too advanced to treat. If the cancer is diagnosed early enough, 90 per cent of the patients can be cured by surgery.

As a footnote to the research, it was also found that women who have a family history of ovarian cancer face a one in thirteen chance of getting it themselves. "We believe these to be sufficiently at risk to justify regular screening," Professor Collins added.

PAINKILLERS

- **Painkillers may make you suffer more**

Painkillers can actually increase your pain if they're used unwisely – that's the warning from an expert.

"When painkillers are overused or misused, this leads to dependence and increased tolerance," explained Dr Steven Brena, director of the Pain Control Center at Emory University in Atlanta, Georgia. "And, when that happens the patient needs more of the medication to get the same effect – and this makes people miserable, frustrated, irritable and anxiety-ridden, all of which increases pain."

He added that even very simple available over-the-counter medicines like aspirin carried the risk of painful side-effects. "People pop these drugs like popcorn, and this can lead to all kinds of problems, ranging from stomach disorders to kidney problems."

PARALYSIS

- **'Brain bridge' may cure paralysis**

An astounding 'brain bridge' may

be able to eventually overcome certain forms of paralysis and also correct some birth-defect problems, says a leading researcher.

"The new technique consists of planting a tiny artificial bridge of millipore, a porous substance, in the brain," explained Dr Jerry Silver, of the department of development genetics and anatomy at Case Western University, in Cleveland, Ohio. "What happens next is that brain support cells – known as 'astrocytes' – attack this implant and replace it, providing a new pathway for blood vessels. This is followed by nerve fibres crossing over this network soon thereafter."

Dr Silver said that the technique has already reconnected two halves of the brain in mice experiments and that this has led him to believe "that we will able to develop similar strategies for humans to correct brain and spinal defects".

using crutches and braces to help them, after the treatment.

"We were very surprised to find such major changes in nerve function just because of a reaction to visible light," reported Dr Judith Walker, director of medicine at the Walker Pain Institute in Los Angeles. "This interaction between light and the nervous system was never known before and we're now studying why and how it happens. Evidently there are nerve fibres alive but dormant that can be temporarily reactivated by a laser. Now we need to find out why they are dormant, why there is a temporary reactivation and whether there could be a long-term reactivation."

Dr Walker added that another study – involving the use of lasers in conjunction with radiation therapy on rheumatoid arthritis patients – was also showing 'encouraging' results.

• Laser beams strengthen paralysed limbs

Laser beams can strengthen paralysed limbs and even help quadriplegics to walk.

The amazing results occurred when laser light was used to stimulate the central nervous system of eight patients who were paralysed from the neck down and six who were paralysed from the waist down. Three from the first group and five of the second were able to walk to a certain extent,

• Phantom pain suggests that brain can rewire itself

Until recently, doctors had always assumed that when a limb was amputated, the nerves leading to the missing arm or leg eventually withered away and died.

A series of studies at the University of California have now shed new light on so-called 'phantom pain', the tingling sensations frequently experienced by amputees and which appear to originate in missing limbs. Seeking explanations of this mystery, the researchers came to the conclusion that the human brain is capable of 'rewiring' itself in such a way that cells no longer receiving stimuli from missing limbs can then be triggered by other brain cells which are getting stimuli from other body parts.

"These findings could prove to be extremely important in the future," said one of the researchers, "as they contribute to a growing understanding of how the brain works and this will help in the treatment of spinal cord injuries, stroke damage, and different kinds of paralysis."

PERSONALITY

• Your choice of dessert reveals your inner you

"You can tell a lot about what your personality is by what your favourite dessert is," says Dr Danilo Ponce, professor of psychiatry at the University of Hawaii School of Medicine, who has made a special study of the subject. And, here are his findings as to what your favourite choice reveals about you:
• If you go for ice cream, you're likely to be creative and artistic as well as being easygoing.
• Choosing pie means that you delight in simple pleasures and tend to live for the moment.
• Cake lovers are outgoing people who like to celebrate and live life to the full.

• If you opt for fruit, you're someone who takes health matters seriously and isn't easily swayed by new fads or unconventional ideas.
• You're likely to have an optimistic and sensitive nature if strawberry shortcake is your favourite after dinner treat.

• What you eat depends on your outlook on life

How you look at life in general is likely to affect your choice of foods, according to a study by the Commonwealth Scientific and Industrial Research Organisation in Australia.

Key findings included:
• If you think you're in control of your life, you're more likely to follow health advice and cut down on fat, sugar and salt while increasing your intake of dietary fibres.
• If your outlook is fatalistic and you believe that you're at the mercy of external events, you tend to ignore dietary advice and just eat what you like.
• Men who worry a lot usually eat more fat and less fibre.
• Tough-minded, aggressive women tend to eat more refined sugar but less salt and protein than others.

• If you're nice, you were born that way!

People who are nice, are so all the way down to their genes, says a recent study of good-natured people, and heredity plays an important part in determining a person's

97

capacity for unselfishness.

Psychologists in the United States found that most instances of selfish behaviour were the result of biological inheritance rather than because of environmental factors.

The strongest evidence for this 'inherited niceness' came from a special study of twins. The scores for empathy and unselfishness were much higher for identical twins than for fraternal twins. Identical twins, of course, share the same genetic inheritance.

PESTS

• Cockroaches can kill!

Everyone is aware that cockroaches are a health hazard, but it has now been discovered that they can even be lethal to some people.

"Many humans are allergic to the common cockroach," says Philip Koehler, a University of Florida entomologist, who is making a special study of the insect. "The pesky creature can even bring on anaphylactic shock, a potentially fatal constriction of the airways and blood vessels that brings on breathing difficulties, rapid heart-beat, falling blood pressure and under certain circumstances heart failure.

"Apart from these rare, but very real, severe risks, we're also seeing that the household cockroach is chock full of things that make people wheeze and sneeze, cough and sniffle, and basically make them feel extremely miserable."

• Pest prevention not to be sneezed at

You can keep ants away from your home by simply sprinkling cayenne pepper where they're likely to congregate – that's the advice in the latest issue of Home magazine in America.

The article adds that you can also stop mice from chewing through an opening by filling it with a rag that has been first soaked in a mixture of cayenne pepper and water.

• How to rid your home of fleas without using sprays

Even the cleanest pets may bring fleas into your home where they can cause a health hazard to you. Here's a remarkably simple method to get rid of those pests without using chemical sprays or powders that in themselves may set off allergies:

• Fill a shallow dish with soapy water and place it overnight on the carpet in the area where you think most of the fleas are.

• Put a small lamp besides the dish so that its light shines directly down on the water. Leave the rest of the room dark.

During the night, the fleas will be attracted by the light, jump up towards it, hit it, and drop back down into the water where – because it has been softened by the addition of soap – they will sink into it and drown.

You will need to do this several nights running initially to get rid of the first batch of fleas and then will have to repeat this at intervals of two weeks until all the fleas are gone. The reason why it has to be repeated is that further fleas will hatch for a while from the eggs in the carpet.

However, two cautions: first, keep your dog, cat or small children out of the room so that they don't knock over the lamp; secondly, make certain the lamp's electrical lead is safe. If you have any doubts about this, you could try using a powerful torch instead.

PMS

• Beat PMS blues by eating starchy foods

Having a starchy snack every three hours or so can help relieve the symptoms of PMS, according to a study recently completed at University College Hospital, London.

PMS symptoms are set off by a lack of progesterone, and this in turn can be the result of low blood sugar levels, according to Dr Katharine Dalton. Starchy foods, however, keep blood sugar levels up and thereby also automatically increase the supply of progesterone – which in turn can lead to a substantial reduction in both the severity and incidence of various PMS symptoms.

In a study of 84 women with severe PMS symptoms, it was found that more than half of these reported a 'marked beneficial effect' when they ate starchy foods – such as flour, potatoes, oats or rice – every three hours. And, for those women concerned about putting on extra weight by eating so frequently, Dr Dalton suggested that they shouldn't increase their total intake of food, but merely divide it into six or seven snacks eaten at regular intervals throughout the day. "We also suggest that women eat within a hour of waking and before going to bed," she added.

POISONING

• Drink can save your life

Alcohol can save your life if you get stung by a Portuguese man-of-war.

"But don't drink it, but instead apply it to the affected areas," explained Dr Elizabeth Sherertz, a professor of dermatology at the University of Florida in Gainesville, who is an expert on jellyfish.

A man-of-war's sting contains powerful poisons that cause painful welts and these can result in fainting, shock and even death.

POLLUTION

• Take off your shoes to stay healthy

It's a good idea to take off your shoes at the front door before stepping in your house, according to French doctor Marc Valchance. "Shoes worn outside can pick up various contaminants and pollutants, such as lead and pesticides, and these can collect in your carpets where they may build up to possibly harmful levels," he explained.

POSTURE

• Three easy ways to a BETTER POSTURE

Stand tall – and you'll look years younger! That's the advice from Dr Jan Perry, a world famous expert on posture.

"Slouching can add years to your appearance because you appear shorter, fatter and burdened down by the cares of life," he asserts. "The good news, however, is that it's easy to correct slouching almost instantly. Here's what you do:

"Stand sideways in front of a mirror so that you can see your full body length in profile – and your ear, shoulder, hip and knee should all be in a straight vertical line. If they're not, just correct your posture by raising your head high, tucking in your chin, and pulling in your abdomen. You'll see instantly a magic transformation taking place . . . and you'll feel better, too!"

Dr Perry, who is chairman of the physical therapy department at the Medical College of Georgia, has also devised a series of exercises which will help you stand as straight as possible all the time:

1) **The Pelvic Tilt:** Lie on your back with your knees bent. Squeeze your buttocks tightly together and suck in your abdomen. Hold this position for a full five seconds, then relax. Gradually over a period of weeks work up to where you can do this up to 20 times without strain.

2) **The Knee Raise:** First do the Pelvic Tilt as above. Then put your hands on your knees and pull them gently towards your chest. Hold this position for a count of ten, then relax. Gradually work up to the point where you can do this up to ten times.

3) **The Upper Back Strengthener:** Lie down on your stomach. Place your hands palms down under your face with your elbows bent. Lift your elbows away from the floor and hold for five seconds. Relax and repeat up to ten times.

Dr Perry suggested that you should start by doing these exercises every second day only at first, increasing this to a daily routine after a couple of weeks. He, however, warned that no one should undertake any exercise programme without first checking this out with their own doctor.

• Good posture can make you TIRED!

It goes against just about everything we've all been taught, but there's now evidence that good posture can make you feel tired.

Explained Dr Robert Fried, director of the Institute for Rational Emotive Therapy in New York: "People who keep their stomach firmly tucked in when they're standing up straight may also be unnecessarily tensing their diaphragm muscles – and this will make it difficult for them to take in a full, deep breath, thereby possibly leading to hyperventilation, that is breathing shallowly and rapidly. That kind of breathing causes an excessive loss of carbon dioxide and makes the blood less able to bring oxygen to the various parts of the body. The net result can be feeling fatigued all the time for no obvious reason."

Apart from creating tiredness, hyperventilation can also bring about anxiety as well as tingling, coldness or numbness in the fingers. There's, however, a quick way to find out whether you're breathing too shallowly: Place one hand on your chest and the other on your abdomen. If both hands don't rise with each breath, you're likely to be hyperventilating somewhat. The cure to the problem, assuming it isn't due to any underlying disease such as diabetes, heart or kidney problems, lies in simple breathing exercises.

PREGNANCY

• No risk to baby if pregnant women work under stress

Contrary to expectations, it has been found that mothers-to-be who work long hours at stressful jobs are not endangering their baby's health.

Researchers in America compared the outcomes of the pregnancies of some 5,000 female medical residents – whose jobs involved long hours and a great deal of potential stress – to those of the wives of an equal number of male residents to find that the rates of complications during pregnancy were roughly equal for both groups. "What's more, the hard-working pregnant mothers had comparatively fewer babies who were under weight at birth than the general population," said the study's director.

• Pregnant women should avoid getting too warm

Women who are exposed to high temperatures during the first three months of pregnancy are up to three times more likely to have babies with birth defects, according to two major studies in the United States.

The sources of heat involved are just ordinary ones like electric blankets, hot tubs and even the overheating that having a fever can produce. All of these, according to reports in the Journal of the American Medical Association and the publication Developmental Medicine and Child Neurology, can have an additive adverse effect. The kind of birth defects most likely to be produced by long-term overheating are especially those that leave part of the brain or spinal cord uncovered by skin and bone.

One of the studies also suggested that the likelihood of these birth defects was also increased if the mother was deficient in beta-carotene, even if this deficiency was not severe enough to produce symptoms in the woman herself.

PROSTATE

What every man over the age of 40 needs to know – now!

Cancer of the prostate is the second most common form of cancer in men. However, if detected early enough, the chances for a cure are excellent. So if you're over the age of 40, the time when the disease usually first manifests itself, these are the signs to look out for that could spell problems:

• A slowing down of the urine stream or force.

• A frequent urge to urinate, most noticed by needing to get up two or three times a night.

• Slowness in starting the stream as well as hesitancy, stopping and starting. A spasm that stops urination.

• Discomfort or pain during urination.

• A sharp pain in the pelvic or rectal areas.

• Incomplete emptying of the bladder.

• Inability to stop the stream, a continuing dribble.

• Traces or stains of blood in the urine.

• Nausea, dizziness or unusual sleepiness. Of course, merely experiencing one or more of these symptoms doesn't mean that you have cancer as there are many other ailments that may be the cause, such as the extremely common condition called Benign Prostatic Hyperplasia, which simply means that your prostate has become enlarged. However, whatever the root-cause of your problem might be, it's always advisable to consult your doctor so that a diagnosis can be made.

PSORIASIS

• Psoriasis sufferers given new hope

Although the dream of a cure for psoriasis continues to elude researchers for the time being, the hope of a more effective therapy with minimum side-effects has become much of a reality with the recent introduction of a brand new form of treatment.

The new compound – called 'calcipotriol' – and marketed in this country under the name of 'Dovonex' is a synthetic analogue of 1,25 dihydroxyvitamin D3 whose chemical structure it closely resembles and was developed by 38-year-old Martin Calverley, a British scientist working for Leo Pharmaceutical Products in Denmark.

Although the structure of calcipotriol is something new, the idea of possibly using vitamin D3 in one form or another to reduce the uncontrolled cell proliferation which is the hallmark of psoriasis had been suggested many years earlier.

Several trials of the new drug – which is used as a cream – have been conducted so far and the results have been extremely encouraging and can be summed up as follows:

• Calcipotriol is clearly of greater efficiency than short contact dithranol therapy, which had hitherto been one of the treatments of choice for moderately severe psoriasis.

• Just about all patients agreed that the new treatment was 'significantly' more acceptable cosmetically than dithranol which can be very messy and smelly.

• Ninety per cent of those treated with calcipotriol had a satisfactory response.

• One in twenty patients required no further treatment.

• Roughly one quarter of those treated did require ongoing maintenance treatment on an intermittent basis after the maximum of plaque clearance had been obtained initially. For those not familiar with psoriasis, it should be pointed out that this percentage of satisfactory response is extremely good and that the need for further treatment for at least some patients was only to be expected as the disorder is a 'waxing and waning' one.

PSYCHOTHERAPY

• Female therapists are better for women

Women who need a psycho-therapist's help will do better if they seek one out that is a woman, according to a recent university survey.

Researchers at the University of California in Berkeley sifted through hundreds of patient records kept by both male and female psychotherapists to find out what terms they had frequently used in describing the progress and treatment of their patients.

"Male therapists were more likely to use words with negative connotations like 'sentimental' or 'cowardly' to describe their women clients," said one of the researchers. "On the other hand, the women therapists favoured constructive words like 'resourceful' and 'appreciative'."

RLS

• Five ways to deal with restless legs

Restless legs syndrome – also known as RLS or Ekbom syndrome – manifests itself in an overpowering urge to keep moving the legs, muscular twitching in the calves, and creeping or crawling sensations in the lower limbs, these symptoms occurring mainly at night. The exact cause of this disorder remains unknown but researchers believe it is triggered by an upset in the chemistry of the brain or by the interference with the passage of electrical impulses through the neurons to the areas affected. Here are some simple tips which could help:

• Take a walk before bedtime to alter chemical balances in the brain by stimulating the release of endorphins.

• Let your feet soak in cold – not iced – water for one minute to lower blood temperature.

• Take a multi-vitamin supplement every day to counter a possible lack of iron that some doctors believe may be responsible for RLS in some cases

• Take two aspirins before going to bed.

• Don't eat shortly before bedtime as it is thought that the digestive process may trigger off RLS.

RISK FACTORS

• The HEART RISKS of being apple-shaped

A woman's shape may affect various aspects of her health, according to the results of a Dutch study published in the British Medical Journal.

Apple-shaped women – that's those whose waists are wider than their hips – are less likely to conceive than those who are pear-shaped with hips wider than their waists, says the study which also claims

that overall shape is more important to fertility than either age or total weight.

There's more bad news for the rounder woman because the survey also revealed that if they are overweight in the first instance, they will find it harder to lose the extra pounds by dieting or exercise.

"And, what's more, they are also at greater risk from diabetes, heart disease and high cholesterol levels," added Luci Daniels, vice chairman of the British Dietetic Association.

SEX

• The penalties of love

The song says that making love 'is quite an art', but it can also be quite genuinely a pain for either men or women as the following two items testify.

WHEN SEX MEANS
A HEADACHE

Thousands of men and women suffer from excruciating headaches while making love or shortly thereafter, a problem known as 'Benign Sexual Headache (BSH)', according to Dr Basil Akpunonu, associate professor of clinical medicine at the Medical College of Ohio, USA.

"The condition is up to three times as common among men than women," he said. "Most suffer in secret from this syndrome because it involves sex and they're ashamed to talk about it. Many people avoid sex entirely rather than seek treatment. And, that's a great shame, because BSH can be quite easily treated with drugs."

Although the basic cause of BSH is unknown, it is believed that it is linked to the rapidly increased flow of blood to the brain during sex. "People most likely to suffer from this condition are those who already suffer from high blood pressure, obesity, other headaches or coronary artery disease," Dr Akpunonu added. "If you're having this problem, you should contact your doctor who will probably be able to treat you with medication that stops the spasms in the artery walls that trigger off the headaches."

WOMEN WHO ARE ALLERGIC TO SEX

Some women are genuinely allergic to lovemaking and it can literally make them quite ill.

"In fact, the women are allergic to seminal fluid," said Dr Roger Katz, a clinical professor of allergy at the University of California at Los Angeles. "Mild symptoms of this allergy include slight to moderate pain or itching during lovemaking, but severe cases may experience lowered blood pressure, shortness of breath, giddiness and may even go into shock."

The condition can, however, be successfully treated, explained Dr Leonard Bernstein, director of of the Asthma and Allergy Treatment Center at Deaconess Hospital in Cincinnati. "We take a sample of the man's seminal fluid and break it up into its protein components," he said. "After that we use both skin and blood tests to find out to which of these components the woman is allergic. Once that's done, several injections of the guilty component are injected into the woman until she becomes desensitised to it. Our success rate in using this technique has been 100 per cent to date."

• Foods that add sizzle to sex

Increasing your intake of wheat germ, parsley and seafood can boost your sex life, says Jeannie Rose, a renowned San Francisco herbalist.

"All of these foods contain zinc or manganese and this promotes the production of testosterone in the body, thereby increasing your sex drive," she explained.

"However, stay away from sweets," she added. "While sugar may give you a temporary burst of energy for love, it also inhibits the production of testosterone."

SHOPPING

• Dangerous trolleys

Supermarket trolleys are involved in more than 7,000 incidents a year which result in people being treated in hospital, warns the Royal Society for the Prevention of Accidents. And, the injuries are by no means always minor, in one instance an eight-year-old girl was killed after being crushed under a trolley full of chipboard in a DIY superstore. A Health and Safety Executive booklet lists the following potential dangers:

• Defective tyres and wheels which make the trolley difficult to control.

• Tipping over on gutters or kerbs.

• Trolleys overturning with children or heavy loads on them.

• Losing control of the trolley down a slope.

SHOULDER PAIN

• How to beat shoulder stiffness

Stiffness in the shoulders is a common cause of all kinds of aches and pains in other parts of the body. For example, some headaches and certain forms of overall tiredness can have as their root-causes shoulder muscles that are all knotted up.

Sufferers from arthritis are, of course, particularly prone to shoulder problems and there are special exercises that have been devised to help these people keep their joints supple and maintain the fullest possible range of movement. Many of these exercises can also be extremely useful to others who – without having arthritis – do experience occasional stiffness. Listed below is a selection of these exercises which you can adapt to meet your own needs. Do, however, bear in mind that you should never exercise to the point where it becomes painful. If it hurts, stop, but try again another day.

ARM SWINGS

1) Sit up straight on an upright chair without arms or on a stool.

2) Let both arms hang down on either side of you.

3) Swing one arm forwards and backwards in a slow, continuous movement.

4) Repeat the above with the other arm.

5) Repeat with both arms simultaneously.

OUTWARD SWINGS

1) and 2) The same as above.

3) Swing one arm outwards at a right angle away from your body.

4) Repeat with the other arm.

5) Repeat with both arms simultaneously.

6) Repeat the whole sequence up to five times.

ROTATING THE SHOULDERS

1) As above.

2) Lift and rotate one shoulder.

3) Lift and rotate the other shoulder.

4) Lift and rotate both shoulders together.

5) Repeat the whole sequence up to five times.

REACHING FOR THE SHOULDER BLADES

1) As above.

2) Place one hand behind the back and try to reach up to touch the shoulder blade on the same side. If this is difficult – do what you can within the limits of your ability.

3) Repeat with the other hand.

4) Repeat up to five times for each side.

SHYNESS

• Shyness may result in abortion

A recent British report claims that many women may end up having abortions because they were too shy or embarrassed to get the 'morning after' contraceptive pill from their doctor.

"Rather than face the embarrassment of obtaining the pill, these women instead decide to take a chance that everything will be all right," explained a spokesperson. "This, of course, often leads to unwanted pregnancies, some of which are terminated."

Although the morning after pills can cause various unpleasant side-effects – including headaches and nausea – they do cut the risk of pregnancy by between 50 and 90 per cent.

Better and more easily available information could drastically cut the number of abortions – which now stands at 170,000 a year, added the report in The Consumers' Association Drug and Therapeutics Bulletin.

SIDE-EFFECTS

• Driving under the influence of a cold pill?

Taking certain cold remedies and then getting behind the wheel of a car can be just as dangerous as driving under the influence of alcohol, say researchers at the Dent Neurologic Institute in Buffalo, N.Y., USA.

"That is because many cold medicines contain antihistamines which can slow down a driver's reaction time and impair their ability to drive safely – much like alcohol does," explained one of them. "And, swallowing even one dose of an antihistamine-containing remedy can be just like having a few alcoholic drinks before driving." Potential side-effects of anti-histamines – which are used in some cough preparations and nasal decongestants – include: dizziness, blurred vision, tremors, digestive upsets and lack of muscular coordination.

SINUSITIS

• Three top tips to clear SINUSES

Sinusitis – whose symptoms are often mistaken for that of a winter cold – is marked by nasal congestion, lack of energy and post-nasal drip. While severe sinusitis requires strong drugs, such as penicillin, minor instances of it could respond to simpler home remedies. Here are three of them recommended by Dr Andrew Weil, of the University of Arizona, and author of 'Natural Health, Natural Medicine':

1) Nasal douching daily. Mix half a teaspoonful of salt in a glass of warm water. When the ingredients are fully mixed, transfer them into a small shot glass, filling it nearly to the brim. Using one hand to close a nostril, tilt your head slightly back, and hold the glass up to the other nostril. Inhale the warm liquid through the open nostril, then exhale it by blowing your nose gently. Repeat, by alternating sides, several times until most of the solution is gone.

2) Put hot, wet towels over your face for 15 minutes up to four times a day. "This is an excellent home treatment," said Dr Weil, "because it promotes drainage from the nose and increases blood flow to it."

3) Eat food that's as spicy as you can stand it. Garlic, horseradish or cajun spices all help the mucus flow and clear the sinuses.

SKIN CARE

• Don't let winter spoil your SKIN

You can prevent your skin from becoming dry in the winter months by following a few simple rules, says Dr David Harris, a clinical professor of dermatology at Stanford University, USA.

"The reason why you may suffer more from dryness in the winter is because humidity which normally keeps the skin plump is low and this may cause irritation, roughness and chafing," he explained. "Here's how to avoid these problems:

"Don't use ordinary soap which can remove the natural oils from your skin, but instead use one that contains a moisturising cream.

"Use a moisturiser lotion before you dry yourself after a shower or a bath. This will add an extremely thin layer of oil to your skin which will help it retain moisture.

"Don't have as many baths or showers in the winter than in the summer because the more you wash, the more you take natural oils from your skin. Using water that's really hot, further reduces those oils."

SLEEP

• Take INSOMNIA more seriously, doctors told

The Royal Society of Medicine has urged family doctors to treat insomnia as a 'medical problem' in itself and not just see it as an unpleasant symptom which may accompany other illnesses.

The recommendation followed a survey which showed that one in seven men and more than one in four women have sleeping difficulties. Stress and worry topped the list of causes for insomnia with 'over-active minds' being blamed by one in eight of those surveyed while another one in ten were kept awake by either pain or illness.

Nearly a quarter of the insomniacs said they became irritable because of lack of sleep and this had caused their relationships with partners to suffer. One in twenty said that they frequently had difficulties staying awake while driving.

One possible cure was suggested by Dr George Beaumont, an expert on sleep disorders: "Get rid of the TV in the bedroom which should be reserved for sleeping. The only other thing it should be reserved for is sex – which can be the best cure for insomnia of all."

• Seven ways to get a good night's sleep

There's nothing quite so miserable as tossing and turning all night in a vain search for the restful sleep that eludes you. But there's good news for insomnia sufferers: anyone can sleep like a log if they heed a few simple tips.

"It's estimated that about a quarter of all people have some complaint about their sleep," says Dr Andrew Monjan, of the National Commission of Sleep Disorders Research in America. "But just about all of these would sleep soundly if they were to follow our suggestions." Here are the recommendations:

1) Have a glass of warm milk just before bedtime. "Milk is high in an amino acid called tryptophan that activates the chemicals in our brain that signal our body that it's time to go to sleep," explained Dr Monjan.

2) Try to be consistent in both the times you go to bed and when you get up. "Don't stay up until 3 a.m. on a Saturday night and sleep to noon on Sunday," he said. "This way you simply won't get to sleep on Sunday night."

3) Do keep your bedroom dark. "Any light – whether it comes from street lights or the moon – will inhibit the production of melatonin, a hormone that helps you go to sleep," he warned. "So use curtains or blinds to ensure darkness."

4) Avoid both coffee and alcohol before going to bed. Said Dr Monjan: "The caffeine will keep you awake and while the alcohol may help you get to sleep, it will disrupt your sleep cycle during the night and you'll wake up feeling tired despite having apparently slept well."

5) Count sheep. "Yes, this really does work," he explained. "Counting sheep stops you from worrying about all of the day's problems by blocking your mind and allows you to drift off."

6) Moderate exercise. "Exercise that's not too strenuous and engaged in at least four hours before bedtime will leave your body pleasantly tired and ready for sleep," he said. "Exercise just before bedtime has the opposite effect and will keep you awake because the body is all keyed up."

7) If sleep doesn't come within 15 minutes or so, get up. "If you don't, you'll just lie awake in bed

worrying about not sleeping," he explained. "Get up, read a book and go back to bed when you feel drowsy again."

• Can't sleep? Read this . . . and this . . . and this . . .

You can get off to sleep fast by using a technique called 'thought jamming', says Dr Kieran Doyle, of the Medical Research Council in Cambridge.

Here's what you do: Pick a word, any word you like, and just repeat it over and over and over in your mind at the rate of three or four times a second. "As you focus on that word, your mind will be prevented from receiving any stimulating or disturbing thoughts and you should drift off to sleep within minutes," explained Dr Doyle. "The technique is simple to use, has no side-effects and certainly is worth giving a try before reaching for the sleeping pills."

• Sleep at work to boost output

If you were to take the occasional catnap while at work, this would probably make you a better and more productive employee. That's the message from psychologist Marty Klein, who heads Syncro Tech, a sleep research centre in America.

"Most people are chronically sleep deprived," he asserted. "Getting enough sleep is not only the single most important factor to doing a job well, but also to our quality of life, health and safety.

"I believe that the solution is to have 15-minute snooze breaks," he added. "Bosses would be well advised to provide rooms where tired employees can take naps. If workers got enough sleep, there would be fewer accidents – and both creativity and productivity would soar."

• The exhaust way to sleep

The gentle purr of a Citroën 2CV engine has cured the insomnia of Les Craze, 37, who runs a garage in Penzance, Cornwall. "I keep a tape I've made of the running engine besides my bed and, when I have trouble getting off to sleep, listen to it and within minutes it will do the trick," he said. "It certainly beats a cup of hot cocoa."

• This might be why you're grouchy

If you often wake up in the morning feeling grouchy and still worn out, it's possible that the cause of your bad night's sleep is right besides you. No, it's not your partner, but it could be an electric alarm clock, radio, or TV, sitting on your bedside cabinet.

Explained Dr William Rea, director of the Environmental Health Center in Dallas, Texas: "All of these electrical gadgets emit electromagnetic waves and these can be a disruptive force in the bedroom and keep you from enjoying a peaceful and uninterrupted rest." Magnetic fields are known to affect people by causing a condition known as 'electro-stress', which may bring about nightmares, sleep-walking and even allergies in those who are particularly susceptible.

Another expert, Dr Andrew Marino, professor of cellular biology and anatomy at Louisiana State University School of Medicine, added: "The risk is real and significant and, depending on the device involved, an electro-magnetic field may still be present when it is turned off." Although the fields are usually very weak, it is believed that they can reach potentially troublesome levels by their cumulative effects over long periods of time as people sleep near them.

The way to avoid any possible problem is simple: just move any electrical gadgets three or more feet away from your bed as most electromagnetic fields drop down to virtually nothing beyond that distance.

• Dracula pill to raise the dead tired

If you have a biological clock that's different from everyone else's, it may soon be possible to 'reset' it with the help of a new hormone pill.

"There are people whose body clocks are out of kilter – they either can't sleep at night or get up at an ungodly hour or are dead tired by lunchtime," explained Dr Lewy, of the Oregon Health Sciences University in America. "We have now found that this clock is controlled by melatonin, a hormone produced by the pineal gland which is a small organ in the middle of the brain. Normally, the body only manufactures this hormone at night and production stops abruptly just as soon as we are exposed to light.

"By giving someone a small dose of the hormone it is possible to delay or advance their wake-up time, depending upon when we apply it. For example, we can fool the brain into thinking it is bedtime when the sun is still shining outside." It is hoped that the new treatment – which has been dubbed the "Dracula" hormone – will be useful in providing relief for jet lag. It has already been successful in regulating the daily rhythms of totally blind people who cannot respond to the visual cues provided by day and night.

SLIMMING

• Want to lose weight? Eat alone!

One way to lower your intake of calories is by the simple expedient of eating alone rather than in the company of others.

So says Dr John M. De Castro, a professor of psychology at Georgia State University, who added that:
• People who eat by themselves –

whether at home or in a restaurant – tend on the average to take in about half the amount of fat and calories than those who dine in a group.

• The solo eaters always spend much less time at the table, thereby removing themselves from the temptation of having more food much sooner.

Unresolved is the question of whether eating alone makes you eat less or whether eating as part of a group makes you eat more. Dr De Castro favours the second explanation: "People who eat in groups may fail to heed internal hunger cues, eating more than they would do otherwise."

• The iron way to SLIM

If you're a woman and are having trouble shedding the pounds despite a vigorous exercise programme, the problem could be that you're deficient in iron.

That's the conclusion of Dr Henry Lukaski, a US Department of Agriculture physiologist, who discovered the hitherto unknown link between iron and fat during tests at the Human Nutrition Research Center in Grand Forks, North Dakota. During the tests, Dr Lukaski deliberately reduced the iron levels of 11 women volunteers and had them train on exercise bikes while he measured their energy output. Then he brought up the subjects' iron levels with supplements and tested them again while they

exercised. And, the results showed that:

• Women with low iron levels were not able to burn as much energy during 'mild to moderate' exercise, burning five to eight per cent fewer calories than when the iron levels were normal.

• And, when the same tests were conducted under 'strenuous' exercise conditions, they burned less fat when low in iron than when their iron levels were high.

"Many women – something like 10 to 15 per cent of the general population are iron deficient, and this is particularly likely to occur during the childbearing years," explained Dr Lukaski, "while this happens to only about one per cent of men. If you're a woman and having difficulty losing weight, have your doctor check your iron level with a simple blood test. If it's low, they may recommend a supplement or a diet plan that's high in iron which may help you in your weight-losing programme."

• Those thin breadsticks can make you fat!

If you're on a diet, beware of bread-sticks! That's the warning from nutritionists at the University of California at Berkeley, USA. Explained one of them: "Breadsticks look thin and inviting and you might be tricked into thinking that they're not too laden with calories and so just might feel safe nibbling a few now and then. The fact is, however, that most store-bought breadsticks are made with oil and many of them have sesame seeds – a concentrated source of fat – sprinkled on them. The net result is that if you eat three sesame seed breadsticks, you'll have taken in 150 calories, of which 42 per cent came from the 7 grams of fat in the sticks."

• When you eat affects weight gain

If you want to lose weight, eat as much as possible of your food intake for breakfast. That's the implication of a study recently completed at Oklahoma State University.

The survey discovered that people who ate 2,000 calories a day over a week lost weight when those calories were mainly consumed at breakfast. On the other hand, another group which took in most of their 2,000 calories at their evening meal gained weight.

SMELLS

• The smell of success is sweet

People work better when their environment smells good.

During a study at the Rensselaer Polytechnic Institute in Troy, New York, 120 students were given various mind-intensive tasks, such as proofreading typesetting or solving word puzzles.

Half of the students worked in rooms that had first been sprayed with apple-cinnamon or light floral air fresheners; the others worked in rooms that hadn't been freshened. When the results of the tests were analysed, it was found that those working in the scented area had outperformed the others by a staggering 25 per cent. "We believe that these results were obtained because the right kind of fragrance counters the negative effects of stress by creating an environment that boosts the mood," said one of the researchers.

• The sweet smells of desire?

The power of smells to arouse passion has been well documented, but many may wonder at the latest instant 'aphrodisiac' for it reproduces the odour of armpits. Its developer, Dr George Dodd, of Warwick University, has however no reservations about the product's desirability and usefulness for he believes that it could help the lonely find a partner and even reduce the ever increasing divorce rate by prolonging sexual desire.

Another view of body smells was expressed in a recent survey for Gillette of the extent of toiletries used in Britain. Their researchers, who discovered that the average male spent £80 a year on toiletries and devoted 23 minutes a day grooming himself, concluded that an ordinary 'man who smells clean' was sexier than one with bulging muscles who didn't.

SMOKING

• Giving up smoking doesn't have to make you fat

The idea that stopping smoking will automatically make you fat is a myth.

That's the conclusion reached by health experts who have recently completed a study of 37 women, aged 18 to 45, who gave up smoking for at least a month.

The researchers at the Department of Dietetics and Nutrition at Queen Margaret College, Edinburgh, found that:

• One third of all the women who gave up smoking had put on little or no weight after six months.

• The average weight gain for those who did experience one was just under five pounds.

• The heavier a woman's smoking habit had been, the greater her weight gain, if any.

• After six months, nearly half of the subjects still weren't smoking and in most cases their eating habits which had undergone a change when they stopped smoking had settled down.

The researchers pointed out that the weight gains that did occur were the result of the subjects eating more and not because of any change in their metabolic rate – which determines how quickly energy in food is burned up. Research fellow Mary Cursiter pointed out: "A lot of women think they are doomed to putting on weight because they will fall victim to this effect, but there was little change in the daily rate of our subjects.

"Some six months after stopping smoking, the metabolic rate does appear to slow down somewhat," she added, "but craving for food, especially sweets, should have eased as well by then.

"Weight gain is not inevitable," stressed Ms Cursiter. "For women tempted into substitute eating, dieting is not the answer – they would probably find it too difficult. My advice is to concentrate on giving up smoking first and not think of dieting until at least the worst of the withdrawal symptoms are over."

• Nicotine patches should carry health warning?

Although nicotine patches and chewing gum have proven useful in helping people to stop smoking, they can constitute a health hazard in themselves, according to a study carried out at The Centre for Biological and Medical Systems at Imperial College, London.

Researchers found that wearing the patches or chewing the gum could cause the blood to flow more quickly through the arteries – an effect similar to that of smoking – and that this could lead to a build-up of fatty deposits and an increased risk from heart disease, especially for those people who already have a heart condition or angina. Commented one researcher:

"The idea is to wean people off cigarettes and this is not a bad way to do it, because while the users still get nicotine, they at least are not receiving carcinogens. But maybe there should be warnings on the packs about heart disease."

• Watch that carrot – it may be addictive!

When smokers are trying to give up the habit, they are frequently advised to nibble something – like a carrot, for example – to ease the pangs of withdrawal.

Now comes the warning that vegetables, too, can be rich sources of nicotine. Says Dr Edward Domino of the University of Michigan: "It's not only carrots that provide nicotine, as potatoes and aubergines are equally guilty. In fact, eating five ounces of mashed potatoes is the equivalent of the passive smoking you'd do if you were to spend three hours in a smoke-filled bar."

SNEEZING

• The facts about SNEEZING

Did you know that a sneeze travels at more than 100 miles an hour? Or that the most common time to sneeze is when you get up in the morning?

These are just some of the fascinating facts about sneezing that have been collected by Dr Guy A. Settipane, an American professor of medicine. Here are some more:
• You shouldn't stifle a sneeze as the rush of air creates tremendous pressure at the back of the throat and this could blast germ-laden particles into your inner ear. In fact, you could even damage your eardrums.
• The reason we say 'Bless you' when someone sneezes is because our ancestors believed that their souls could leave their bodies when they sneezed.
• Contrary to the popular belief, you heart doesn't stop when you sneeze. A sneeze's purpose is to rid the body of foreign invaders in the nose, such as pollen or dust, by a sudden dislodging blast of air.
• Commonly we sneeze in a series of bursts rather than just the once.
• Some people have been unable to sleep or eat because they sneezed so often and have had to be hospitalised for treatment.

• If you SNEEZE a lot, blame your parents

If you suffer frequently from bouts of sneezing – the chances are that your problem is hereditary.

A study has found that 64 per cent of children whose parents sneeze a lot are also frequent sneezers. This suggests sneezing sensitivity is part of genetic inheritance, say researchers L. Beckman and I. Nordenson, of the University of Umeå in Sweden.

SNORING

• Stopping snoring

There's now a quick cure for chronic snorers. Experts at Papworth Hospital, Cambridge, have perfected a procedure which uses a laser on the throat to permanently stop the snores. To date, 20 patients have been treated and none has so far relapsed. "What's more, we know that curing the snorer in one instance saved his marriage," said one doctor. The operation is done under a general anaesthetic and leaves the patient with a sore throat for a few days, but there are no other side-effects.

• The electronic cure for SNORING

An amazing electronic device that 'cures' snoring has been credited with saving marriages plagued by this problem.

The anti-snore machine was developed by Dr Raymond C. Rosen, professor of psychiatry at New Jersey's Rutgers Medical School, who said: "We've had an 80 per cent success rate in reducing snoring to a level where the spouse is satisfied."

This is how the device works: A microphone records the snoring sound and when this reaches a preset level of loudness it sets off a switch that wakes the offending sleeper. The snorer then presses a button to switch off the alarm and reset the machine.

"Each time the snorer becomes too loud, the machine wakes him up again," explained Dr Rosen. "Gradually, the snoring will lessen both in frequency and intensity, and when this happens the device can be adjusted to respond to snores of lower and lower volume.

"This device has already proven extremely useful in marriages troubled by snoring," added Dr Rosen.

SORE THROAT

• Tips for a SORE THROAT

You may find that the following homespun remedies may help if you've got a sore throat:
• Keep your mouth closed and breathe in through your nose as that way the air you inhale will have been slightly warmed before it reaches your throat. Breathing through your nose also helps remove impurities from the air.
• Gargle with half a tablespoonful of salt dissolved in a glass of water. This will help wash away surface germs which may be causing the soreness.
• Humidify your bedroom as some sore throats result from sleeping with the mouth open, thereby parching the delicate tissue.
• Raise the head of your bed as some sore throats can be caused by stomach acids backing up and causing irritation.

• Treat yourself to a new toothbrush – your old one may have collected bacteria which are causing the soreness.

• Gargling with hot water which has some salt dissolved in it may also help, as can slowly sipping hot lemonade.

Of course, if the throat is very sore or the symptoms persist, you should see your doctor.

SPRAINS

• The RICE way to treat a SPRAIN

If you suffer a sprain, treat it with RICE, says Dr Joseph F. Fetto, associate professor of orthopaedics at New York University Medical School. The 'rice' he recommends won't however be found at a take-away restaurant, and is instead an acronym denoting Rest, Ice, Compression and Elevation:

• **Rest:** Stop using the injured limb immediately.

• **Ice:** Apply this to the injury as quickly as you can to stop inflammation from spreading. You should apply the ice for about a quarter of an hour, then remove it for half and hour, then apply it again for a quarter of an hour, keeping up this sequence for the next day or two.

• **Compression:** This helps reduce swelling and is best done with an elastic support bandage. Begin by wrapping the bandage below the affected area, continue over the ice pack, and finish off above the injury. Don't overdo the tightness of the bandage, however.

• **Elevation:** When you're not using the ice pack, keep the injured area higher than your heart level. Depending upon the injury, you can do this by using pillows to prop up an arm or a footstool for a leg.

Although most sprains can be successfully treated at home, you should always consult a doctor if you don't feel any pain from it as this could indicate nerve damage; or if the pain and swelling are severe or persist.

SQUINTS

• Lethal poison can uncross eyes

A deadly bacterial poison – the toxin botulinum, which causes sometimes fatal botulism – is being used to correct children's crossed eyes without surgery.

In the new technique – developed at Duke University Medical Center in America – the toxin is injected into the muscles surrounding the stronger eye where it temporarily paralyses it, thereby relaxing the eye and allowing it to uncross. The effects of the toxin normally last about three months during which the cross-eyed condition is usually fully corrected. Should the problem persist, the injection can be repeated.

STIFF NECK

• Butterfly pillow may ease STIFF NECK

If you often suffer from a stiff neck when you wake up in the morning you may get relief by sleeping on a 'butterfly' pillow which allows your head and neck to rest in their natural position on your shoulders when you're lying down in bed.

Here's how you make such a pillow: use an ordinary soft pillow and wrap a few strands of wool around its middle so that you end up with a butterfly shape. When you go to sleep, place your head lying across the waist of the pillow with your neck supported on both sides by the 'wings'. Place your butterfly pillow directly on the bed and don't raise it by putting a bolster or under-pillow beneath it.

STOMACH CANCER

• Simple test can pinpoint STOMACH CANCER risk

Half of the cases of stomach cancer – a major killer disease responsible for 8,000 deaths a year in Britain – may be the result of a simple infection that could be treated easily in its early stages.

It has been known for more than a decade that the bacteria Helibacker Pylori – often just called 'HP' – frequently plays a major role in the subsequent development of stomach or duodenal ulcers and that dealing with the bacteria also clears up the ulcers. Recently, however, it has been demonstrated that the HP infection can also later lead to stomach cancer with people having it in a persistent form being up to six times more at risk.

Researchers found that sufferers from stomach and duodenal ulcers often had HP infection and that this at times led to pre-cancerous changes in the lining of the stomach. Once the infection was cleared – usually by a course of bismuth or omeprazole as well as antibiotics – the lining returned to normal. And, experts believe, when this happens, the previously increased risk of stomach cancer also reverts to normal. This means that if the HP infection can be diagnosed and treated sooner, this should have a massive effect upon the stomach cancer death toll, perhaps cutting it by as much as half.

STOMACH ULCERS

• Horsefly extract can cure ULCERS

Horsefly stings contain a substance that can cure ulcers and other stomach disorders – that's the claim of researchers at the University of Pavia in Northern Italy.

Professor Mario Pavan, an insect specialist who heads a team that's been working for years with various insect venoms, stated: "The common horsefly secretes a substance in its sting which can eliminate injury scars as well as treat ulcers.

"We found this secretion most beneficial when used on rats," he added. "Injections of it caused the animals' coats to glow with health, and in one rat, a scar on its back vanished completely. This led us to try it on human patients and surgeons experimenting with it at two Italian hospitals found it could eliminate post-operative scars.

"We then discovered the secretion's power to treat ulcers and have now tested this on humans with an injection aimed at the ulcer so as to dissolve the offending tissue build up. So far, patients who volunteered for the initial trials have all reported excellent results."

STRESS

• Power naps reduce STRESS

If you're under a lot of stress, a power nap could do you a world of good. That's the recommendation of anti-stress expert Dennis Shea, of St Luke's Hospital, in St Louis, Missouri.

"A power nap is just like an ordinary nap," he said, "but it's called that because it revitalises your power for the rest of the day. Ideally, you should take your power nap during mid-to-late afternoon and it should last about 20 minutes or so. Anyone who is under a great deal of stress will find that this is extremely beneficial as a natural lowering of the body rhythms takes place during napping, allowing you to start the second half of your day fully refreshed.

"You should, however, be careful not to overdo things and restrict your power nap to an absolute maximum of 30 minutes, as longer than this could interfere with your night-time sleep cycle."

• Sex victims of the stress doctors

Many young women end up sleeping with their psychologists, the very people who are supposed to be helping them through emotional traumas – that's the shock finding of a survey of almost 600 NHS psychologists which showed that one in fifteen admitted to having become sexually involved with a patient either after or during therapy.

"People abused in therapy have increased experiences of anxiety, depression, an inability to trust other people and have a tendency to suicidal feelings and acts," commented Dr John Marzillier, chairman of the Professional Affairs Board of the British Psychological Society.

Eight psychologists were investigated for abusing patients in the last year, and five of them resigned before the inquiry was completed. Now the Society has asked Health Secretary Virginia Bottomley to increase their powers of disciplinary action.

• Talking is women's favourite way of beating STRESS

A good natter is women's favourite way of relieving stress, according to a survey of nearly 600 cases conducted by Dr Janet Griffith, of Columbia University School of Nursing in New York.

But how women choose to cope with stress varies according to age – for example, more than half of the young women interviewed said they sought to solve their problems by discussing them with friends. Women aged between 55 and 65 years, however, generally preferred ignoring a problem or seeking relief from worry in drugs or alcohol.

Over all the age groups, the most common ways that the women dealt with stress were: talking it over with friends, 48 per cent; immersing themselves in work, 38 per cent; religion, 31 per cent; overeating, 29 per cent (the percentages add up to more than one hundred because many women used more than one way of alleviating their stress).

SUBLIMINAL

• The truth about learning tapes

Do learning or self-improvement tapes which carry subliminal messages designed to reach the listener's subconscious really work?

No, definitely no, according to a study just completed at the University of California during which 78 men and women listened daily for five weeks to tapes with such messages as "I have enormous concentration ability" or "I like myself and others". Before listening to the tapes, the volunteers were subjected to a battery of tests that measured both their memory and self-esteem – they were tested again at the end of the study and none had improved in any way.

SUGAR

• The sweetest remedy

Sugar can do a better job of treating seriously infected wounds than the latest space-age drugs – so say a number of American doctors who have tested it on a variety of patients.

And, in case you have any doubts about this, the sugar in question is the plain granulated variety that you'll find in just about any kitchen.

"Plain sugar heals seriously infected wounds that even the most modern antibiotics can't cure," says Dr Richard Knutson, of the Delta Medical Center in Greenville, Miss., USA. "When I first heard of it 15 years ago I was treating a patient who had incredibly resistant bedsores. We tried all kinds of antibiotics, but nothing worked.

"Finally, a retired nurse who was working with me recalled that some

30 years ago she used to put sugar on wounds with success. I decided to give it a try.

"Incredibly, it worked! In fact, it was so successful that I kept on using it, mixing the sugar with a mild bacteria-killing iodine liquid. Since then I've used this treatment on more than 6,000 patients with anything from burns to shotgun wounds."

Sugar's wonderful curing power was also endorsed by Dr B. G. Spell, of the Methodist Rehabilitation Hospital, in Jackson, Miss., who said: "I use sugar every day to help heal infected amputations and the pressure sores that plague paraplegics."

Commented Dr Mary McGrath, divisional chief of plastic surgery at the George Washington University Medical Center in Washington: "Sugar does heal wounds. It's been successfully used through the centuries, and can still be used safely today."

The key to sugar's success is simple: the granules absorb moisture from the wound thereby killing off bacteria by denying them the water they need to survive. This curative power was known to the ancient Egyptians who used sugar-rich honey to treat wounds.

• Sugar doesn't make you FAT

It's always been assumed that eating too much sugary food could easily make you fat, but scientists are now having to reconsider that proposition in the light of recent research.

A team of Swiss researchers led by Professor Eric Jequier of Lausanne University has discovered that the fattening effect of sugar is much less than had been believed until now because it was found that the body uses up carbohydrates, sugar and starch within 24 hours and only one per cent of it turns into fat.

Previous studies about sugar's fattening effect had been based mainly upon tests conducted on laboratory rats whose livers are much more efficient at making fat from sugar than those of humans.

So the word is: sugar may help rot your teeth, but it's not a grave threat to your waistline!

SUICIDE

• I'm so lonesome I could die

Sad country songs may be instrumental – no pun intended – in driving lonely people to kill themselves.

"People who are going through a suicidal crisis could be pushed over the edge by listening to country music," claimed James Gundlach, a sociologist at Auburn University in Alabama, who recently co-authored a research paper on the subject.

The paper– entitled 'The Effect of Country Music on Suicide' – said that these tunes tended to convey a sense of hopelessness. What's more, most country music lyrics dealt with lost love, financial strains, despair and marital difficulties – all of which, said the authors, were ideal to nurture a suicidal mood.

The authors started their research when they found that there were unusually high rates of suicide in Nashville and Oklahoma City, both country music strongholds with the most common victims being young white men of working class background.

• Suicidal tendencies may be inherited

The tendency to suicide is partially hereditary, according to American researchers who have completed a massive study of the subject during which health investigators looked at the records of 243 psychiatric patients with a family history of suicide.

They found that more than 48% of those patients had attempted suicide, and that 84.4% had a depressive disorder at some time. Doctors then compared these patients with more than 5,000 others who had no family history of suicide to reach the conclusion that such a history is "definitely associated" with significant increased risk.

SURGERY

• To shave or not to shave, that's the question

The common procedure of shaving the body area before an operation may actually increase the risk of infection by damaging the skin's outer layer and thereby promoting bacterial growth, claims a report recently published in the United States.

Surgeons are now looking at better ways of removing body hair and some studies have shown that abandoning the traditional blade razor in favour of clippers, hair-removing creams or electric razors, resulted in a lower rate of postoperative infection. Some doctors are also of the opinion that in many cases of surgery there is no need to remove the hair surrounding the incision site at all.

TATT SYNDROME

• Feeling tired all the time?

A recent British study of 1,000 adults revealed that nearly 50 per cent of them frequently felt tired for no immediately evident reason. And, this epidemic of listlessness is particularly sweeping the country's go-getters, according to the researchers.

Unlike the so-called Yuppie Flu (Myalgic Encephalomyelitis), the new TATT (that stands for Tired All The Time) syndrome doesn't affect people badly enough to stop them working, but it does impair their performance. Sufferers are, however, warned that they shouldn't just soldier on, but should see their doctor if the problem persists.

"Don't ignore it," is the warning from Cary Cooper, a professor at

Manchester University's Institute of Science and Technology, whose subject is occupational stress. "The tiredness is possibly masking an underlying problem. If you go on ignoring it, you may develop symptoms like migraine or gastric problems. The thing about stress is that you don't grab your heart and keel over, instead the body starts to warn you by making you feel tired, indecisive and depressed."

As to where all the extra stress was coming from, he commented: "We have a new work ethos nowadays that puts people under enormous stress. To this you have to add the recession and fears of job losses."

TEETH

• Prevent tooth decay by eating the right foods

Eating the right foods can make a major contribution to preventing tooth decay and gum disease – and some of these foods can even help damaged teeth repair themselves.

That's the claim of Dr Susan Harlander, of the University of Minneapolis School of Dentistry, who explained that plaque, the bacterial film covering the teeth, converts many carbohydrates into acids that cause decay. "But decay-fighting foods prevent the plaque from producing these acids or at least reduce the rate at which the acid is made," she said. "The damage wrought by the acids can also be reduced by stimulating the

flow of saliva in the mouth." Foods that particularly stimulate saliva – and thereby help neutralise acid – include: lemon juice, cherry flavouring, mature cheeses, as well as most substances that are tart or sharp-tasting. Another expert, Dr Ralph Margulies, suggested that you can also retard tooth decay by following a balanced diet and that you should "eat a lot of protein, especially at breakfast, as this helps neutralise acid formation."

The specific tips offered by the experts are:

• Cheeses best for fighting cavities: Swiss, aged cheddar, mozzarella, gouda, blue, and brie.

• Other foods high on the list: peanuts, walnuts, ham, and eggs.

• Choose whole grain foods as the effort required to chew them is good for the gums.

• Fresh green salads help because they act as a detergent on the teeth.

• Be sure that your vitamin C intake is adequate because it increases the blood flow to the gums and jaws and also strengthens the blood vessels supplying them.

• Tea is a natural cavity-fighter because the average cup of tea has three times the fluoride content of ordinary water.

• If you must have a snack, avoid the sugary and starchy kind and have a carrot or a banana instead. It has been demonstrated in laboratory tests that eating bananas or carrots causes the bacteria on teeth to stick together and this can make it easier to brush or floss the germs away.

• Tea is good for your children's TEETH

Giving your children a cup of tea may help them avoid tooth cavities - that's the discovery announced by Dr Memory Elvin-Lewis, of the Washington University School of Dental Medicine, St. Louis, Missouri.

"Tea works its wonders in preserving teeth because it contains three times as much fluoride as an equivalent amount of fluoridated water," said Dr Elvin-Lewis. "Our research has shown that children who eat lots of sweets, but also drink a great deal of tea, have fewer cavities than those who don't have tea."

Tea gets its fluoride as the growing plants absorb it from the soil, the doctor explained. Incidentally, instant tea has a higher fluoride content than the brewed kind and there's almost no fluoride at all in most herbal teas.

• We'll soon be able to grow NEW TEETH

Within the span of a generation or less, men and women of all ages will be able to grow a third set of teeth. That's the stunning claim by dental experts at the University of Lower California, who base their forecast on pioneering cloning experiments, which are expected to make artificial tooth enamel for filling cavities available within the next five years.

"And, once that breakthrough takes place, it will pave the way for the eventual total restoration of teeth within less than a decade thereafter," said dental consultant Dr Jonathan Long. "This will mean that a new set of teeth can be grown at will . . . and even a fourth or fifth set as needed."

"The artificial enamel, which will have properties equivalent to, or better than, normal human enamel, will be cloned from genetic material that is inserted in yeast," added Dr Harold Slakin, a biochemistry professor at the University. "We have already taken the initial step towards identifying genetic material that would cause the yeast cells to manufacture the protein molecules for the enamel and it is now only a matter of time before dentists will be able to carry out total teeth replacements."

• Cold in the nose can trigger toothache

If you've got a pain in teeth in the upper jaw, the cause may well be a cold in the nose. Researchers have discovered that the cold can spread from your nasal passages into the sinus cavity above the jaw and so cause swelling that presses painfully on the nerves connected to your top teeth. You feel as though you've got a toothache, but the cure for the pain, of course, is to treat the cold in the nose.

• Chewing vitamin tablets can decay your teeth

Vitamin C tablets can at times be a useful adjunct to your diet, but don't chew them – because that could cause your teeth to rot.

According to Dr John Guinta, of Tufts University, in Medford, Massachusetts, USA, the frequent chewing of vitamin C tablets can completely erode your teeth over a period of time. "The problem," he explained, "is that in some people vitamin C promotes an unduly high buildup of oral acid, which quite literally eats away the teeth."

However, there is no need to forgo your vitamin tablets. "Just swallow them with water instead of chewing them," Dr Guinta advised.

TONGUE, BURNED

• Quick cure for BURNED TONGUE

If you've burnt or scalded your tongue by eating food or drinking a beverage that's too hot, you may find that sprinkling a few grains of sugar on it can help, and should relieve the discomfort within minutes. Apply more sugar some time later if still necessary. Of course, this home remedy is only meant for minor burns, as a severe scald or burn requires medical attention.

TOOTHPICKS

• All you ever wanted to know about toothpicks

FIRST, THE GOOD NEWS:
Toothpicks can give you healthy gums by controlling plaque and bleeding.

Dr Martin Weinstat, a San Francisco dentist, has made a special study of toothpicks and how they're used and these are his recommendations for the most efficient technique:
1) Wash your hands.
2) Rub your fingers along the gumlines.
3) Hold the toothpick with the thumb and forefinger, keeping your other fingers curled up outside your mouth.
4) Gently insert the pick into the gum grooves around each tooth, working from the back of the mouth to the front.
5) Use your right hand to clean the outside grooves of the teeth on the right side of your mouth.
6) Use your left hand to clean the inside grooves of the right teeth.
7) Reverse the procedure described in points 5 and 6 to clean the left teeth.

"If every dentist taught patients to use toothpicks properly, we could wipe out gum disease in no time," asserts Dr Weinstat, who added: "If you find that the gum pocket surrounding any tooth is more than a quarter of an inch deep, see your dentist. Deep pockets are often a sign of advanced gum disease."

NOW FOR THE BAD NEWS:
Toothpicks can be bad for your health – and even kill you – if you accidentally swallow one.

According to Dr Lawrence D. Budnick, of the Centers for Disease Control in Atlanta, some 8,000 Americans end up in hospital each year because of accidents involving toothpicks. And, at least three deaths have resulted from swallowing toothpicks during the past 15 years.

"Children, of course, are the most accident-prone and those younger than five years were found to be 20 times more at risk to suffer severe injuries from toothpicks because at that age they're prone to stick the sharp picks in their eyes or ears. Toothpicks should definitely be kept out of the reach of very young children."

UNEMPLOYMENT

• Losing your job can kill you

Studies commissioned by the US Congress' Joint Economic Committee have revealed that losing your job can be harmful to your health and lead to everything from mental and physical illness to divorce and even death.

The studies found that:

• Getting fired increases the risks of depression and anxiety, insomnia and loss of self-esteem.

• People cut down on good nutrition, causing an increase in various ailments.

• After a year of unemployment, heart attacks and strokes in men aged over 45 reach their highest point.

URINARY INFECTION

• Cranberry juice fights urinary infection

Drinking cranberry or blueberry juice has been recognised as a time-honoured popular home remedy for urinary tract infections – and now science has confirmed that it really works and they have also discovered why.

Researchers at the Weizmann Institute of Science in Rehovot, Israel, say that both juices contain a special compound which prevents bacteria from adhering to the bladder. Other fruit juices were also tested, but only the cranberry and blueberry varieties contained the infection-fighting compound.

• Vaccine for urinary infections

Scientists are very close to developing a vaccine that will protect women from chronic urinary tract infections, known as UTIs.

An experimental vaccine consisting of several dead bacteria strains was recently used in a trial at the University of Wisconsin when it was injected into the vaginas of 22 women who suffered the disorder.

Over the next five months, nine of the women had either no outbreak of infection or only one. Without the vaccine, the statistical expectation was that they would have had at least two or more each. "This is really very good news," said one of the researchers, "and it shows that it won't be long now until we have a vaccine that offers complete protection against UTIs."

VASECTOMY

• No side-effects
Having a vasectomy doesn't put you at greater risk from heart disease, cancer or any other major illness.

The good news comes from researchers who studied the health records of more than 10,000 men who had vasectomies and compared them to an equal number of men who hadn't had the operation. Commented Dr Gerald S. Bernstein, of the University of Southern California: "The results don't support any of the previous suggestions of long-term problems, including in particular heart disease, developing after a vasectomy."

• Vasectomy without an incision
A unique 'no scalpel' technique for performing vasectomies is undergoing trials in the United States after having proven effective in treating more than ten million men in China.

The procedure – developed originally in China in 1974 when the population explosion there created a need for a quick, simple way of reducing the birthrate – involves making a very small hole in the scrotum, removing the vas deferens and sealing off the ends of the tubes with a special needle that produces scar tissue.

Early American tests suggest that the technique, being less invasive, reduces bleeding and is also less likely to lead to subsequent infection than the conventional vasectomy procedure which requires an incision in the scrotum.

VEGETARIANISM

• Vegetarian children are not healthier
One would perhaps have expected vegetarian children to at least be less overweight if not necessarily more healthy than their counterparts eating a normal diet, but that is not the case according to the preliminary results of a survey of 120 nine-year-olds in the North-West.

Not only were the vegetarian children just as likely to be overweight as the others, but they were also found to have slightly less energy, reported Dr Alan Hackett, of John Moores University in Liverpool, who headed the survey. He added: "We are about to explode the idea that the vegetarian diet is necessarily healthier."

VIDEO GAMES

• What's the truth about video games?
Many parents are worried about the amount of time their children spend

playing video games. And, this concern reached new heights recently following several incidents where children had suffered fits resembling those associated with epilepsy while playing video games. Now many such games are to carry health warnings stating that their use could cause epileptics to experience altered vision or mental confusion. While this move has been welcomed by concerned parents, other questions about the possible health hazards of video games remain either unanswered or the subject of controversy within the medical profession.

This is what the experts had to say on the subject:

• "Children playing video games could be increasing their risk of heart disease because they aren't getting enough exercise to lower their cholesterol," said Dr Neil Armstrong, of Exeter University. This view was echoed by the American Academy of Pediatrics who said that children who watched TV, an activity similar to playing video games but not quite the same, for more than four hours a day were more than four times as likely to have high cholesterol levels.

• American researchers claimed that overweight children could burn off more calories by playing video games than by taking a stroll as the excitement of playing caused heart rates, blood pressure and oxygen consumption to be raised. Another study of 16 to 25-year-olds found that their energy expenditure increased by 80 per cent and their heart rates went up by 25 per cent while playing.

• "Video games have some very strong, positive impacts on children," declared Dr Geoffrey Loftus, a psychology professor at the University of Washington, D.C., who maintained that the games helped in various ways: by providing a boost to the children's self-esteem when they won; teaching problem-solving skills; improving eye-hand coordination as well as mental concentration; and promoting family interaction by bringing old and young members together to play.

• A much more sombre warning came from Dr Dieter Korczak, a German sociologist, who said that teenagers who spent hours playing video games could turn into sex freaks. "Sexually these people lose interest in taking time to make love properly," he asserted. "They just want quick satisfaction. Everything has to be mega-byte fast." His remarks are perhaps backed up to a certain point by the sex crime statistics from Silicon Valley, America's computer belt, where they are well above average.

So, are video games bad for your children or not? It looks like we'll have to wait a while longer to find out. In the meantime, most experts cover their bets by saying that there's no real risk providing game playing is indulged in 'in moderation', leaving parents to define for themselves exactly what that means.

VITAMINS

• How to get more out of vitamins

Millions of people are wasting their money on vitamins because they take them on an empty stomach, say researchers.

"Many vitamins have to be taken at the same time as food, or they will do you no good at all," claims Dr Howard Lutze, of Washington, D.C. "These include vitamins A, D, E and K. And, it's not enough to just have a light breakfast, like a slice or two of toast, to make them most effective. You need to eat a substantial meal like hot cereal or eggs."

Another researcher into the effects of vitamins, Dr Hank Newbold, of New York, adds that B-complex and C vitamins should be taken at intervals spaced throughout the day and not all at once.

"One of the biggest mistakes made by many people is taking vitamin E and iron at the same time," he explains. "This is just about a complete waste of time and money, because the two counteract each other. What you should do is to have your vitamin with breakfast and take your iron around lunchtime."

Both experts also say that for maximum benefit calcium supplements should not be taken with a meal. On the other hand, raw fruit eaten at the same time will reinforce the effects of zinc, selenium or any multi-mineral supplement.

• Eat right to think better

What you eat determines how well your thinking processes work if you're past the age of 60, according to a recent study.

Research at the University of New Mexico has shown that even mild nutritional deficiencies contribute to a deterioration in the mental ability of older people with those getting less than the recommended intake of riboflavin, folic acid, vitamin B12 and vitamin C performing poorest in tests.

• How vitamins got their name

Most of us know that our bodies need 13 essential vitamins to be healthy, but here are some fascinating facts about those vitamins:

• The VITA in vitamin means life in Latin. And AMIN comes from the word 'amine', the name that early scientists gave to a group of chemical compounds believed to help prevent scurvy and other diseases.

• Originally, each identified vitamin was given a letter to denote it rather than a name. Later, what was thought to be one vitamin was discovered to be several – such as, for instance, the vitamin B-complex.

• Most vitamins are quite similar in that they're made of the same elements: carbon, hydrogen, oxygen and nitrogen. However, these elements are arranged differently.

• Three different vitamins - folic acid, pantothenic acid, and biotin – were all originally known as vitamin M. Confusion is eliminated nowadays by using chemical names.

WARTS

• Mind power can cure WARTS

You can use the power of your mind to cure warts – that's the amazing conclusion reached by two separate studies, both of them at Carleton University in Canada.

In one survey, ten people were told under hypnosis that they could use their imagination to make their warts shrink. Another ten had their warts treated with salicylic acid, a commonly used remedy.

"At the end of six weeks, those who had been hypnotised had lost an average of 54 per cent of their warts," reported Dr Nicholas Spanos, who headed the study. "The people in the salicylic group hadn't lost any warts at all."

In a second study, Dr Spanos compared the results obtained when 64 people were divided into groups. Twenty-two subjects were hypnotised and told that they could eliminate their warts by daily sessions of imagining them beginning to tingle, then growing warm, and eventually disappearing The other volunteers were given what they thought was laser treatment, but in fact was a fake.

"At the end of six weeks, the hypnosis group had lost 34 per cent of their warts," said Dr Spanos, "while those treated with the 'laser' had lost a mere nine per cent."

WEATHER

• Why the weather can make you sick

The weather can definitely affect your physical well-being for better or worse.

That's the conclusion of Dr Lawrence Armstrong, assistant professor of exercise and environmental physiology at the University of Connecticut.

"Summer heat makes us lethargic by affecting the body's circulation," he asserted. "There is, however, little we can do to counteract this when we're outdoors.

"Sudden changes in the weather pattern also adversely affect many people," he added. Until recently, it had always been assumed that this was because of the alteration in barometric pressure, but now researchers believe that people are instead reacting to the fluctuating

130

balance of negative and positive ions in the air.

WHIRLPOOLS

• The dangers of a WHIRLPOOL

Having long dips in a whirlpool bath can be hazardous to your health, according to Ian MacArthur of the Institution of Environmental Health Officers.

He explained that some bathers who had been using badly maintained pools had suffered infections, nausea and soreness due to the harmful bacteria that can breed in the warm water.

"We advise people to have dips that are no longer than 20 minutes," said Mr MacArthur. "The longer you're in the bath, the longer you're exposed to potential contamination."

WINE

• Why red wine is good for you

Although it has been accepted for some time now that red wine drunk in moderation can provide some protection against heart attacks, there has been controversy among experts as to why this should be the case.

The definitive explanation for wine's prophylactic effect has now been discovered by scientists at Israel's Volcani Centre at Bet Dagan: the answer lies in the wine's non-alcoholic components, in particular, substances called phenolic flavonoids which have potent anti-oxidant properties and discourage fats from furring the arteries by blocking the oxidation of fats in the blood.

This may serve to explain why the French – who eat a great deal of fatty food, but usually wash it down copiously with red wine – suffer a great deal fewer heart attacks than we do, a phenomenon that for years has been known as the 'French paradox' to cardiologists.

WORK HAZARDS

• How to beat the pain of being desk-bound

Sitting too long in one position – which is something that many workers can't avoid – can cause all kinds of pains and aches.

However, according to experts, you can beat most of these nagging pains – and stop them from striking again – by doing some simple movements that help pump the blood more efficiently through your body.

"Sitting for a lengthy time in one position stops the blood from circulating properly in the legs causing them not to get enough oxygen – and this can trigger off discomfort and cramps," explained Dr Herman Hellerstein, professor of medicine and cardiology at Case Western Reserve University in Cleveland, Ohio. "The heart is a long way from our legs, so it can be difficult for it to pump blood back up the legs when muscles in the lower legs are relatively inactive.

"The simplest way to get the muscles moving and the blood pumping, of course, is to get up and move around – but sometimes that isn't possible because we're stuck at our desks, strapped into an airplane, or just trapped in our car. But, even in those situations there are little things you can do to help yourself . . ."

• Lift your heels by contracting your calves while keeping your toes on the floor. A sequence of these heel lifts – done at the rate of about one every three seconds or so for a few minutes – will squeeze large veins inside the calf muscles and help pump blood back to the chest.

• Tightly tensing the muscles in the upper thighs for a second or so and then relaxing them – and repeating this sequence a dozen or so times two or three times and hour – is also extremely useful.

• And, for those who have to stand up for long periods of time, shifting your weight from one foot to another will promote the blood circulation in the lower part of the body.

WORRY

• The more you worry, the more you sleep

People who sleep less than six hours a night are probably less worried, less anxious, and more outgoing than those who sleep more than nine hours a night.

These are the conclusions of Dr Nicholas Skinner, of the University of Western Ontario, Canada, who compared the personality traits of 'short sleepers' with an equivalent number of 'long sleepers'.

"The short sleepers – who average 5.7 hours a night scored 13.9 on a test designed to reveal the most extroverted personalities," he said. "This compared with a score of 12.2 for the long sleepers whose sleep averaged 9.5 hours. Even more revealing were the results of a test to measure anxiety levels – the short sleepers scored only 9.9 while the long sleepers scored 13.2."

These results contradict previous findings which had concluded that anxious people tended to wake up early in the morning.

WOUNDS

• New superglue can bind WOUNDS

Surgical stitches – and the scars they can produce – may soon be on their way out thanks to a new type of biological adhesive which makes it faster and simpler to seal wounds and incisions.

"The treatment is instant so you don't distort the tissue, and scar formation is thereby reduced," said Dr Alan Roberts, of St Luke's Hospital, Bradford, West Yorks, where the superglue was developed over eight years. The new technique is currently having its final tests and is expected to be available shortly.

• New bandages fight infection

Bandages that can fight infection by using built-in disinfectants have been developed by Japanese researchers.

"These bandages should be especially useful in treating burn patients, who are particularly susceptible to infection," said Dr Tomiki Ikeda, of the Tokyo Institute of Technology, adding that "traditional bandages need to be treated with antibiotics to repel infection."

The disinfectant is chemically bound to the gelatin-like film of the new bandages and is released at a controlled rate over a period of several days. "The disinfectant is likely to do a better job of warding off infection because it is made from synthetics, not natural materials like antibiotics to which germs are more likely to develop resistance," added Dr Ikeda.

WRINKLES

• Almond oil can delay wrinkle formation

Almond oil – which you can get at most health food shops – is said to help soften the little lines and wrinkles that form around the eyes and mouth if a small amount of it is gently massaged into the problem areas once or twice a day. However, be very careful not to get any of the oil into the eyes themselves.

XLA

• New hope for XLA babies

The gene responsible for a very rare disease which leaves its victims without an immune system has been identified by doctors at Guy's Hospital in London.

About 40 babies a year are affected by the disorder which only affects boys and is passed on by chromosomes from the mother. The identification of the 'guilty' gene means that it may eventually be possible to use gene therapy to cure sufferers and that carriers of the disease can be pinpointed.

Something like 300 people in Great Britain have XLA. This makes them extremely vulnerable to any kind of infection with potentially fatal results. Current treatment consists of infusions of antibodies every twenty days so they can remain alive.

YAWNING

• Why yawning is so terribly good for you

Yawning may be considered impolite in some circumstances, but it's really a wonderful exercise and pick-me-up.

We have all been taught to suppress our desire to yawn, forgetting that this is probably the fullest kind of breathing possible when we need extra oxygen as well as a good stretch of the facial muscles.

When you yawn you automatically contract and relax various muscles around the jaw, teeth, cheekbones, face, and eyes, which is a lot better for them – and you – than keeping them tightly clenched.

Research has shown that a good yawn or two or even more immediately brings the following benefits:

• As you breathe in extra air, fresh oxygen flows to the body cells.

• It will help you wake up in the morning while, on the other hand, prepare you for restful sleep at night.

• It relaxes the muscles in your midriff and can help cure indigestion.

• Your eyes will feel better as the muscles surrounding them are contracted and relaxed, promoting the production of natural tears to soothe them if they're tired or dry.

And, extra benefits are to be gained if the yawning is accompanied by a good stretch of the neck, shoulders, back and arms. So stop being inhibited about yawning – the desire to do so is your body's way of telling you that it would like a bit of extra oxygen and that a good stretch of the muscles wouldn't be amiss either. By the way, if circumstances allow, don't stifle the noise the yawn might make – the more you open your mouth and let the sound escape, the greater the intake of fresh air.

ZINC

• ZINC supplements could be dangerous

If you're eating a well balanced diet, you shouldn't need zinc supplements and taking them could even endanger your health.

"My study shows that adding excessive zinc to the diet of healthy persons for prolonged periods is clearly dangerous," said Dr Ranjit Chandra, a professor of medicine at Memorial University in Newfoundland, Canada.

Dr Chandra added that although extra zinc could be beneficial to people suffering from some disorders, it could also cause heart and circulatory problems as well as impair the normal functioning of the body's immune system.

He said that the average Western diet provided 10 to 15 milligrams of zinc daily, which was close enough to, or within the range of, the recommended intake. "Anything more than this could be dangerous unless specifically prescribed," he warned.

134

HEALTH TIPS

A NEW BOOK REVEALS VITAL health tips based on the latest nutritional and scientific findings and time-proven remedies. This book is of vital importance to everyone interested in their health. Here are a few tips covered in this *Complete Handbook Of Health Tips:*

- How to get more energy and combat fatigue (3 nutrients may help).
- How to flatten your tummy with a 20 second, daily exercise.
- A nutrient that may help improve memory.
- How to deal with stress, including what nutrients may be helpful.
- A nutrient that may increase resistance to disease.
- 4 simple ways to take off weight.
- The only effective way to get rid of cellulite.
- A cheese that can help prevent tooth decay.
- A herbal remedy to prevent migraine headaches.
- One doctor's way to prevent grey hair.
- How to get rid of face hair.
- How to shorten the miseries of a cold.
- 3 tips for relieving sinus congestion.
- 5 ways to stop foot odour.
- 3 nutrients to minimise harmful effects of alcohol.
- 2 vitamins that may help avoid bruises.
- 5 ways to relieve haemorrhoids.
- How to relieve nightly leg cramps.
- Prostate trouble: A simple tactic to alleviate getting up nights.
- 4 tips to fall asleep faster.
- A nutrient that may help lower blood pressure.
- How to detect and relieve food allergies.
- A tip for preventing car sickness.
- How to prevent bladder infections.
- A vitamin that may repel insects when taken orally.
- A simple technique to relieve tension.
- How to relieve dry skin.
- 4 tips to avoid food poisoning
- How to stop snoring.
- 3 ways to avoid stomach irritation when taking aspirin.
- 4 vitamins that may be harmful if taken to excess.
- 6 aids to eliminate constipation.
- 7 suggestions to relieve heartburn.
- A safe, simple home treatment for sore and tired feet.
- How to relieve bloating and puffiness.
- A common food to reduce cholesterol
- 10 tips to ease back pain.
- Latest research findings on the good effects of vitamins, minerals and other nutrients.

You can order the book direct from the publisher for only £9.95 *(fully inclusive)*. To order, send your name, address and book title with payment (cheque or Visa/Access) to Carnell Ltd, Dept. HH1, Alresford, nr. Colchester, Essex CO7 8AP, allowing up to 14 days for delivery. You can return the book at any time for a full refund if not completely satisfied.

≋MOPS≋